BEYOND REPAIR

BEYOND REPAIR

Living in a Fractured State

•••

SEBASTIAN MATTHEWS

Red Hen Press | *Pasadena, CA*

Library of Congress Control Number: 2020938865
ISBN: 978-1-59709-436-8

Printed in Canada

The National Endowment for the Arts, the Los Angeles County Arts Commission, the Ahmanson Foundation, the Dwight Stuart Youth Fund, the Max Factor Family Foundation, the Pasadena Tournament of Roses Foundation, the Pasadena Arts & Culture Commission and the City of Pasadena Cultural Affairs Division, the City of Los Angeles Department of Cultural Affairs, the Audrey & Sydney Irmas Charitable Foundation, the Kinder Morgan Foundation, the Meta & George Rosenberg Foundation, the Albert and Elaine Borchard Foundation, the Adams Family Foundation, the Riordan Foundation, Amazon Literary Partnership, and the Mara W. Breech Foundation partially support Red Hen Press.

First Edition
Published by Red Hen Press
www.redhen.org

to Vievee

to Curtis

Contents

He is looking for what he loves, he tries to
capture it. It's found anywhere, everywhere.
Those who are not hunters do not see
these things.
—Robert Henri, *The Art Spirit*

They meant exactly what they said. It was
only that they spoke another language.
—James Baldwin, "Equal in Paris"

I have the impression that thinking is a form
of feeling and that feeling is a form of thinking.
—Susan Sontag, *Rolling Stone*

Rounding the Curve

A year out from our accident, and everyone asks, "So are you all better?"

I wince theatrically and give a *more or less* sign.

"Maybe eighty percent..." Though really some days it's more like fifty.

"Well, you look fine," they say. "You wouldn't even know..."

Yeah, I think. *How about that?*

I'm in Chattanooga, about to head home; it will take a little over three hours across the mountains back to Asheville. I probably shouldn't have come, but I wanted so bad to *connect* with people again. I'd become, out of necessity, something of a hermit, yearning through those many long months of rehab and recovery to return to a life before everything changed—back to my body, my writing life, my family, my friends.

On my first day in Chattanooga I went walking, heading out across the long, wood-planked boulevard that spans the wide Tennessee River: the center of a trio of bridges. The late afternoon light painted the sky a backlit blue screen riffled by breeze. Bicyclists drifted by. A parade of bodies thronged the bridge, each body bathed on one side by sun glaze. No one was in a rush, no one on his or her cell. And I kept walking, off the bridge and into the city, letting my mind take snapshots inside the massive tombstones of commerce it floated through. (Without realizing it, I asked a blind man for directions, and he pointed the way.) Soon enough I was passing back out onto a bridge's arching spine; and, for a few moments, I was back fully in my body—floating atop an island of trees—in perfect balance, attuned to everything around me.

Sunday morning I wake to birdcall and the plaintive whistle of a far-off train. Lying in the dark, I assess my condition. Left hip tight. Body stiff and achy. Right leg a little weak, a dull pulse in the femur at each break. Left foot a block, stiff at the ankle, as though someone has strapped duct tape over the top of its arch and pulled tight. Even my rib cage makes itself known with a tiny blare of pain at the sternum where it hit the steering wheel. Getting dressed in the dark, balance slightly off, I sway a little putting on my jeans, nearly falling over. A quick cup of coffee before slipping out of my friend's dilapidated Victorian. Mincing my way down the cracked stone steps.

Two hours into the drive home it starts to rain. Waves of gusty wind roll in. The traffic narrows but doesn't slow . . . and now I am shaking like a ragdoll behind the wheel, surrounded on both sides by lolling big rigs. Afraid I am going to lose control of the vehicle, I pull off at the Newport exit. There's an abandoned gas station just down the road; I park the car around back, let the seat down, and shut my eyes.

I open my eyes. A car is driving straight at us. I close my eyes. I smell the smoke pouring through the shattered windshield. I open my eyes. A grim-faced EMT is hovering above me.

"We're going to have to pull you from the car, sir."

I've been stuck behind the wheel for close to an hour, feet jammed up under the dash, only my ragged breath keeping me tethered to the earth. Ali and Avery have been sent to the hospital via ambulance. Ali is badly injured and our eight-year-old son, Avery, has walked away with seatbelt burns. I don't know this yet, but the man who hit us suffered a heart attack, dead before his car drifted over the centerline into our lane.

Pull you from the car, sir.

My eyes open. Close. Open. A second EMT is leaning into the open door. Together the two men take hold of me, cradling me in their arms. Then they wrench me up and jerk me a quick left out and away from the dash. I scream. Black out. I wake up in the whirling roar of the helicopter lifting off the ground, on its way to the nearest hospital as storm clouds gather.

Certain experiences draw up the sudden impact. Bumping my head. The sound of tires screeching. A crowded hall or sudden loud report. That specific burnt tire smell. With each, a part of me returns to the scene. All the classic PTSD symptoms—triggers sending me into quiet panic mode, raising my heart rate, or shutting down any emotional response. Flight, fight, or *freeze*.

We live by a public golf course, and one morning, an errant golf ball careened into my windshield. I shouted out of fear, banging the wheel in rage. I shouted again. *Fuck, fuck, fuck.* Later, when I explained to Avery that ever since that ball hit the windshield I'd been jittery, he said, "Dad, you've been jittery ever since the accident."

For a long time I resisted the hard truth of not being able to fully return to my old life. A traumatic event such as ours cleaves a life into *before* and *after.* You have to climb into a new life, hand over fist, one foot in front of the next. Recovery is less about return, or repair, than it is about re-creation. You must retrain yourself to enjoy life, to engage in it without fear.

The rain has stopped. A few hours erased. I edge the car out of the lot and onto the business road. No way in hell I am getting onto that highway. Instead, I turn up a back road and probe for a route through the mountains, gripping the wheel tightly on the steep grades and switchbacks. When I come upon a detour at a downed bridge and have to turn around and find an even smaller road to ascend, I swallow hard and retrace my route. I keep moving forward through the drizzle and fog. I drive mile after slow mile, passing tumbledown barns, a lonely horse in a corner of a tiny field, and a fast-filling river— up and up until I finally crest a ridge, atop one of the gaps this part of the country is famous for, high above the forested hills.

I pull over at the scenic overlook, and while I stare out into the valley, I think of the home I am heading back to. Ali will be getting ready for dinner. Maybe Avery is playing soccer with his friends. The dogs will be eager for a walk. I can take a shower and grab a quick nap before I join Ali in the kitchen. It will feel good to be back in our new, albeit tentative, routine.

These images bring with them a recollection: the first time after the accident that I bathed standing up. I remember stepping tenderly into the upstairs shower . . . after months in a wheelchair, then lugging a walker . . . I was free-standing, head down, floating around the little steamy bubble like a sunflower, the water just a notch under scald. It was a brand of free agency I had all but forgotten—an easy physicality in the body, an eager wakefulness to sight and sound.

And, in turn, this feeling carries with it a vivid memory of being eighteen, on my own in Senegal, returning to my host family after a day of wandering the Dakar streets, notebook and camera wrapped in a satchel. I'd do my teenaged best not to nod off at dinner (fish and potato stew, bottles of Coke at each place setting) then head upstairs for a shower. Standing naked in that room, as skinny as I'd ever been after a bout of something vaguely malarial, I felt incredibly alive, entirely alone. A sink against a concrete wall, a small unframed mirror hanging over it; a shower head propped up in one corner; the tile floor slightly tilted in at four angles, drain in the center; and a rectangular window high up on the other wall, with a view down on a neighborhood I had to tiptoe in order to see . . . The smell of evening fires, "Beat It" blasting from an old-model car . . . I'd stand under that ragged spray for as long as I felt I could, not wanting to take someone else's hot water. I was inside and outside at the same time. In body, out of body. Happy, sad. Wildly alive and a little dead inside. And I wanted to extend that beautiful reset: the dark outside pulsing with layers of insect trill and car horns, and, underneath, domestic sounds from the neighbors wafting up through the window.

I pull back onto the road, a loose CD pushed into the slot, and now mellow reggae is seeping like heat from the speakers, the bass pulsing in the sun. The road winds south then west then southwest—and I am breathing in and out, deeply, as I did back in that locked-up car seat, pressed against that wheel. It saved my life then—*literally*, a doctor pointed out months later—and brings me back to my body, stilling the panic, placing me in my seat, in my hands and feet, lifting the haze that fogs up in my eyes. And it's not long before I am electric again on the switchbacks. I drop down the mountain road through a cheering crowd of trees as Marley chants, allowing the wind and rain to wash over me. And, coming through a tunnel blasted through the mountainside, I am unafraid again, even a little adventurous, in love with unencumbered movement, the slight resistance in the wheel . . . just a little spurt of speed banking the turn . . .

When we think of a unified or singular American identity, we lose the chance to truly understand ourselves and one another.

—Kazim Ali

White Men in Trucks

What is it about them that shoots a brief goose of fear into my blood-stream? Is it imminent threat sounding in the revved engine? Derision caught in the side-view mirror? Or plain old disdain drumming its fingers on the drivers' side door? A little of each?! All I know is I am walking through our suburban neighborhood, and a truck barrels past, not slowing nor moving over. That another swerves around the bend, almost clipping my dog, meeting my upraised hands with a jutting middle finger. And another drives right up behind me and rides my bumper all the way up the hill.

Just yesterday, downtown Asheville, a man steps around me in line and interrupts the conversation I'm having with an acquaintance. He is showing me a photo of his five-year-old boy holding up a large fish caught in one of the Biltmore ponds.

The man steps in closer. "That a bream?"

He's got a smile on his face that I read as hostile. He wants me gone. But the father ignores the man, finishing his sentence about the peaceful water and how quiet it is out there with his boy.

"Almost mystical," he says.

The man interrupts again, smile getting bigger. "Hey, Mike, that a bream your boy is holding?"

Mike bursts into an equally large smile.

"Hell no," he drawls, and lists all the fish his boy has or could have caught.

I don't fish, so I don't follow. Nor can I make clear sense of the quick-fire exchange. The two men have fallen into a bravado-fueled, friendly back-and-forth—it's as if they're flashing each other signs or showing each other their good-old-boy badges. I feel as though I am being erased from the moment, *No Trespassing* signs staked at my feet. The men chat and laugh in the corner as I slip back in line.

Later, at dusk, one more truck appears; it slows to a crawl and follows me up the street. What's with people these days? Are they so sick of their lives that they need to lash out at strangers? To hate them for being something foreign or different?

I turn to face my nemesis, who has rolled down the window.

"Whadya want?"

The man smiles, remains silent. There's power in a comfort with silence.

"How old is that dog of yours?" he asks, leaning out the window.

He's talking about the lab, just a puppy, bounding over and standing up as if seeking the man's arms. The man laughs. The look in his eyes is pure sadness.

Determined

She is famous among those who pay attention. Famous for walking back and forth along Tunnel and River Roads. She roams as far out as Bee Tree and far into town as the Asheville Mall, maybe further. That's at least a ten-mile range. You can see her striding along the edge of the road most every morning and again in the afternoon. There's something about the sight of her on the side of a road that hardly anyone dares to walk—handbag clutched to her side, blonde-white hair cut in a wedge atop her head—that you find strangely affecting. It's hard to tell exactly, but you'd say she's in her early sixties. Tall. Spine straight. Once, in a heavy rain, you pulled over and asked if she wanted a lift. She didn't look at you, her face hidden, a quick shake of the head in the negative. You've heard this is the case for other people who have tried to lend her assistance. Is it fierce pride? Necessity? You never see her looking weary or exhausted; even when she is moving slow, there is steadfastness demonstrated in her gait, a one-foot-then-another brand of doggedness. Often, she's almost speedwalking—her free arm swinging out jauntily, stride elongated a couple of notches—and in those moments she looks almost happy, as if she becomes her fullest self inside her strides. You assume she is going to work, maybe at one of the big box stores. Though lately you've come to believe she never stops walking, like the mythical shark that never rests. That maybe she is making that loop endlessly, from the mall to home, home to mall. Or maybe there is no home. Or she never makes it to the mall. Maybe she is doing it for those who notice such things, who have come to believe she is conveying something of the utmost importance.

Useless

Dodgeball Night at Avery's middle school. Two girls who look like sisters oversee the ticket table in front of the gym doors. I've paid with a twenty, but they only have singles. Someone's mom pats Avery on the head as he walks inside.

One girl struggles to count out the bills so the other takes over the task.

"You're useless," I tease.

The girl's face crumples in shame for half a second then recomposes, replaced by a stoic frown.

I've blown it. *Useless* is what parents say to children, teachers to students, boss to worker, coach to player. You can't catch, can't count, can't spell, can't do anything right.

"I'm just joking," I say, leaning forward. "I'm the one who is useless."

I try again.

"Really, I kid like that all the time."

A dozen bills get handed back.

Avery has returned, looking for me.

"Isn't that right? I tease you all the time."

Never one to comply for compliance's sake, Avery shakes his head. "No, you don't."

The mom has come back over, a worried look blooming. I stuff two singles in the tip box as hush money and hurry inside.

At the Waterpark

The sudden downpour that cleared the decks has packed up and moved on. The sun blares down. The speakers blast Counting Crows's "Mr. Jones." Families troll past in swim trunks; teens move in small packs on the lookout for a brand of adventure they won't find here. The young lifeguard moves so deeply inside a bored loop—eyes scanning the empty pool in a prescribed route—that I worry after his mental health.

The young man (white) behind the fast food counter laughs with two young women (white and Asian). He has drawn a picture of the Asian woman, who says, "The eyes are too small."

The other woman tells the teen, "If you draw me, I'll slap you."

When the first woman turns to a task, he alters her drawing, showing it to his coworker. "You're mean," she says.

He balls it up and throws it away, laughing. When he sees me watching him, he freezes, throwing me a look that is both a shrug and a sneer, daring me to say something.

This is my first time since the accident bringing Avery and his buddies to this park. I'm entirely out of my element here—uncomfortable, socially awkward, snobbishly put-off. I have always hated this brand of tourist experience, sure, but now I really hate this place—how suburban American it all feels, how canned. Hate how everyone seems to be living vicariously through their children or starts acting like them. I'm entirely unable to just go along for the ride. For all those reasons and a few more, I tend to overdrink the park's overpriced booze. Tend to sit in corners and read books. To walk the periphery of the property and explore the off-limit truck bays, the parking lots and empty stairwells. Eventually I give in, slip on mirrored sunglasses, and tube down The Lazy River, observing the sunscreen-slathered families bob and float, listening to the parents talk down to their children.

Back at the bar, a sixty-something woman with a mountain twang speaks up. She barely fits on her bar stool; she's so small. "I used to weigh four hundred pounds," she says, taking a swig of her super-sized margarita. "I just keep shrinking."

Then it's just me and the bartender—J. Crew catalogue handsome, slick, friendly.

"I'm just saving up money to get back to Prague," he confesses, arms across chest.

"What's there?"

"My girlfriend. She wants me to marry her."

"Will you?"

He acts as if he's thinking it through as he surveys the scene.

"Not sure. It depends on what sidles up to the bar."

I call bullshit. "Really?"

He smirks as he wipes down the counter.

"I'll probably marry her."

Eventually, the boys come find me at the bar. They are thinking of joining the line for the Vortex, egging each other past their cartoon fear.

Avery says, "I heard if you don't weigh enough, you'll get stuck."

His friend laughs. "That's okay, there's a hatch."

AWOL

. . . on a flight from Charlotte to Newark

The young Marine stows his carry-on bag in the overhead compartment before sitting down in the aisle seat. He keeps the shiny, white-peaked utility cap on his lap. The flight attendant asks if she can put it in the overhead bin. The young man politely refuses and places the cap under the seat in front of him, arranging his feet around its pristine edges. His hair is dark black, his skin long-winter pale.

I don't know what gets the young man talking, but soon he is telling me that he is stationed in North Carolina, on furlough for two weeks to visit family back in New Jersey. That he is recently divorced. I ask how long the marriage lasted. He bows his head and mumbles, "Not long."

He talks at length about the difficulties of living on base as a young married couple; how his ex-wife got lonely and went AWOL.

"If she's holed up where I think she is, well, you might see me on TV."

He looks directly into my eyes before fiddling again with his headphones. He takes his Coke from the stewardess, smiling politely when she hands him the cup and napkin.

"Really, I am a pretty calm guy."

When I ask him what size family he's returning to, he smiles, listing off its members.

"Mother, sister, younger brother, a couple of cousins."

There's a long beat. "And my father . . . I guess."

A few more beats: "He's a nice guy when he's not drunk."

Turns out his dad is a firefighter, or was one *until he drank himself out of a job*. He was six years from retirement, on his way to being chief. My seatmate leans down and shifts his cap a little. Later, as the plane begins its gradual descent, the young Marine tells me more about his life in the service, about how he often serves as his platoon's designated driver.

"I drink," he says, "but only a beer or two. I just turned nineteen. I watch myself."

Lately, he says, they have been training for cold weather action. He looks proud.

"I am used to the heat. Not sure about the cold, though. I get shivering pretty fast."

When I ask him whom he wants as our next president, the young Marine frowns, lips pursed. He puts on his music and disappears into it, eyes closed.

Near the end of the flight, everyone's awake, preparing to disembark. I ask the soldier about women in the Marines, thinking of the two women officers I just read about who completed the special ranger training. He doesn't answer at first.

"It's biological," he says, as we wait for the plane to taxi to the gate. "Men are programmed to take care of the female first."

He shifts in his seat. "And I am not saying it's right. But it's true."

I don't know what to say to that.

"And there is no place for that in battle. There's a protocol."

The young man shakes his head sadly, and carefully lifts up his cap, placing it in his lap. He puts his headphones back on and blasts music until the line starts moving. When it's his turn, he stands up and retrieves his bag. I watch him inch forward to the door, fixing the cap on this head, and I worry for his ex-wife's safety.

Odd Jobs

I am driving Avery home from school when he asks, semi-seriously, "Dad, do you even work?" I have to laugh. "I mean, what exactly do you do all day besides read books and type on your computer?" (At three, Avery asked "Dad, why you are always writing on paper?")

I try to explain the project I'm currently working on. How I am documenting the encounters I've been having with the people around me; how it seems, in the time it has taken to heal from the head-collision, that the whole world has changed course. And how I feel like I have moved out of my own PTSD-state only to walk out into another, larger, traumatized realm.

I look over at Avery. He has stopped listening, turned into his phone and another YouTube video.

I sit down later and write out every odd job I've ever worked, starting from delivering papers and babysitting, through waiting tables and bookstore clerking, all the way up to adjunct teaching. If I can't convince my son I actually work now, at least I can show him that I worked in the past. When he gets home from school, I sit Avery down and read him the list. He tells me he gets the picture, but I make him listen to the whole, long list.

Somewhere along the line, I bought the idea that a writer must become, in the words of novelist Henry James, "one of those on whom nothing is lost." That I must become a multi-directional microphone. Something that picks up all the surround sounds—a camera capturing the unfolding events, a beat reporter taking notes on the day-to-day in his flip pad. My goal: to see and understand and live inside my life with as much attention as possible. In order to be a real writer, I have convinced myself, I must be open to people—all kinds of people—and must move out of my comfort zone.

But, of course, this approach comes with the potential for some serious blind spots. So many paradigms to recognize and biases to remove. So much energy expended to rise out of complacency. So many risks. And there are days, like today—when the effort of parenting a child seems difficult enough—that such an approach feels nearly impossible.

Blind Spot

Last night Avery needed picking up at Tarwheels, a roller-skating rink one township over. I wanted to get him by ten thirty even though the place closed down at eleven. It was a safe scene, still I worried about leaving a preteen out on his own so late. Even though he knew to stay inside, what would it take for him to break that rule? A couple of cool teens urging him out to take a hit off . . . ?

I headed out right around ten, stopping to get gas. At the register, I noticed an older gentleman hovering by the door. He seemed tuned into my presence; by the time I was done paying, he was standing behind me, in my blind spot.

(Which reminds me, there's this scene in an early episode of *The Americans* in which the Russian spy—disguised as a normal, suburban American Dad—asks two thugs to get out of his blind spot. He's talking to this badass boss man. They don't move. He asks again, looking nervously over his shoulder. They don't, so he kicks the living shit out of the men. When he's done, he turns back to the boss and says, "I told them to get out of my blind spot.")

So I gave my guy a stare. He waited for me to grab my things off the counter before approaching.

"You going out toward Arby's?"

"I work at the grocery."

He showed me the apron in his hand. "I need a ride back to my room."

My first inclination was to shake my head and walk away. But something told me to give him a chance. So I stared a little longer. He didn't *look* like a serial killer. Actually, he seemed like an exhausted man in need of some sleep.

"Okay, let's go."

The man followed me to my car, climbed in, gave me his name, and sat quietly as we headed east on Tunnel Road.

"You staying at the hotel?"

"At the veterans' place," he said.

"The one across from the Dollar Store?"

"Yeah."

He looked over at me.

"Most people don't know the place exists."

"Well, I've lived in the area a while."

"It's good," he said, "to know where things are."

A few minutes later, we pulled up outside the hotel. The man got out, thanking me as he shut the car door. I watched him join a gathering in the well-lit lobby.

When I got to the roller rink, Avery was waiting for me at one of the tables next to the video games. He looked exhausted.

"Let's go," he said.

He skated wearily—and gracefully—to the car. I drove home, passing the vets in their fishbowl, letting the song on the radio serve as talk.

A Problem

I am sixth or seventh in line, in that familiar post office slowdown mode. One old guy looks to be sending a huge tube to some far-off country, in need of insurance and insurance on top of the insurance. Another poor soul counts out change at a glacial pace. All I need are a few stamps.

One woman comes back and cuts in line to tell the clerk that she smells something burning in the lobby. He looks up, unperturbed, and says, "I'll check on that shortly." I bump up a few more spots in line. The tube guy has one more thing he needs to ask. The man behind me sneezes into the kink of his arm.

Three, four minutes pass. I peek out the window, as if catching a glimpse of my car changes anything. One of the clerks puts up a closed sign by his window, off for a break. The first clerk looks up absentmindedly and says, to no one in particular, "I better check on that fire."

Mine aren't the only pair of eyebrows raised.

A gruff "Next!" brings me to the counter. The postman is surrounded by packages, stacks of envelopes. He wears a rubber tip on his thumb. The heels of hands are smudged with ink. I am not a regular at this branch, so there's no nod of recognition, no brief banter. *A book of stamps, please.* He reaches for the stamp folder with a sigh, takes a peek at the clock. *Whatever you got.* A sheet—not a book—placed on the counter, then the fast succession of key punches, the recitation of price. He takes my twenty dollars without looking up and reaches into the open drawer for a ten-dollar bill and, with his pointing finger, scoops out two dimes from the change dish. *No receipt, thank you.*

You'd think in this post-9/11 world there'd be a little more collective concern, but when I reach the door, Tube Guy is still chatting away with the clerk, who still hasn't torn himself away from his tasks. The empty lobby smells vaguely of burnt paper. I push open the door and head for the car, step picking up ever so slightly. Not my problem.

Selma

for V.

King has just accepted the Nobel Peace Prize, and now four school-girls are walking down the steps of a church, deep inside their lives, cradled inside the building, walking and talking and laughing. My friend leans over in her movie theater seat and whispers, "You know what's going to happen, don't you?"

And I am not thinking but then I know, in a split second, that these are the girls in Birmingham, and I avert my eyes just as the bomb goes off, and when I look again windows are exploding and the girls are thrown in the air, over the bannister. And as the camera lingers on the carnage, the dead bodies, I start to cry, devastated by the act, but also out of relief, for my friend has tried to save me from another blind head-on crash inside the head, one more shell-shock moment.

Whenever King sits next to a window, I wince and wait for a brick, or a Molotov cocktail, to come flying through the window. (How can any-one live with that much death hovering outside the window?) Every time a protester gets slammed to the ground by a cop, or a man or wom-an gets punched in the face or knocked into a wall or billy-clubbed or shot in the stomach, I understand that I am meant to make some sense of the violence, the hatred enacted, to feel it in my bones.

When the marchers are met on the bridge with a wall of hate and vitriol, my friend and I hold hands and take the beatings full on. Neither of us cares to step back from fear. I don't want my own shell shock to keep me from the painful truths of our world. Isn't that al-ways the fight? Not to slip into sleepwalking. Not to be overwhelmed and shut down in boredom or abject fear. Not to let fatigue and de-pression and dread bring you down. Not to let overload and triggers shut me down. To walk up onto that bridge, hand in hand, or sit at the desk by the window and face down anything that threatens to bring us down.

"Crippled"

"The last time we saw you, you were a cripple."

This from the wife of an old writing pal. She was right about not seeing each other for some time—going on four years—but it was the *crippled* part that turned my head.

Later, at the conference reception, she seemed open, friendly even. Had she just been stating what she saw as the plain truth? "We weren't sure you were going to get out of it," she said. Get out of what? The rut I was in or the wheelchair? "Here I am," I said, meaning for better or for worse, like it or not. "You were like family," my pal said later, when I confided how much their hospitality had meant to me back then. Past tense. *The last time we saw you . . .*

I was saved by an old student—a "kindred spirit," was how he put it. There was a look of genuine worry on his face, forward-facing questions. And so, thankfully, I leaned into those.

Trauma tends to paralysis. The traumatized are struck, as in shock, into inaction in a posture of wordless gaping.
—David Baker

Her Hair

A disheveled woman somewhere in her early sixties is standing inside the elevator. She seems confused or, at least, in the middle of a perplexing thought. After a brief hesitation, she steps out and gives you a polite smile. You step in, pushing the button for the main floor. Just as the door is sliding closed, the woman turns back and asks, "Are you going up?"

Something about her voice, her odd question, the familiar smile, makes you stop the closing doors.

"Lost?" you ask, noticing confusion lodged in her eyes. "Where are you hoping to go?"

"My hair," the woman says. She holds her hand up to her head. "My hair."

The woman walks distractedly toward the door that will take her out onto the busy street.

You step out of the elevator and walk after her.

"Were you with anyone?"

This stops her.

"My husband dropped me off," she says as if just remembering.

Then, as if another thought has come to her: "I have Alzheimer's."

This explains things.

"Where are you going?"

Her hand goes back to her hair.

"I don't know."

You feel you need to do something to help.

"Come to the next floor," you say. "Maybe your husband is there."

You know that the second floor opens out to a quiet commercial street, the most likely place for her husband to be.

"Come with me," you repeat.

"Okay."

The woman follows you into the elevator, happy to have a place to go. You push the button for the second floor, and she smiles.

"Ah! Two!"

When the door slides open, you step out and slowly make your way down the hall. There are shops on either side of you. You could be out with your mother.

The woman looks into the windows as if on the lookout for a hand-bag. She stops and points at the window of a hair salon. Her face lights up. "This!"

Of course, her hair!

The woman opens the door and peers in. Her stylist waves her over. Stepping inside, she looks like a child setting out on an adventure. As the door closes behind her, she stares directly at you, a look of recognition animating her face.

The Flags of River Road

It's been over two weeks since the Confederate flag came down off the South Carolina capitol building. Since then, I keep seeing southern crosses in the back of pickup trucks; flag bumper stickers, flag T-shirts; flag murals, flag hats.

The drive from our house to Avery's middle school consists of eleven miles along River Road. The trip takes about thirty minutes, depending on traffic.

The Confederate flags have always been here—in windows, tacked to barns, on license plates—but I find them especially conspicuous now. Hard not to read the recent uptick as a big "fuck you" to anybody who resists this mountain-south brand of white supremacy.

Each morning we pass a nature center and a public golf course, the mall, a woodworking shop named Lothlorien, the county's technical college, an old-fashioned roundhouse in the process of being torn down, a popular rib joint, three hipster dive bars, Zen Tubing, an ancient (supposedly haunted) county jail, and three convenience stores boasting live bait.

Like the *fuck you* from the young man as he backed his truck, fast, on a blind turn, ignoring my honks. He pulled right up alongside me before drifting slowly into a makeshift parking space. He looked over at me and sneered his defiance.

There are at least two river put-ins, scores of nearly invisible houses stuck up in the hills, with old cars parked in precarious places, and at least a dozen churches, including the Freedom Biker Church, which occupies a dilapidated storefront next to an empty Aikido studio, across from a plastics plant.

This morning I watched my neighbor turn out onto River Road too close in front of an advancing car: having to speed up to avoid getting rear-ended, my neighbor was punished for his transgressions by the guy tailgating him around the bend.

A willow tree's branches hang over the road, bangs cut straight.

The flag needs to come down, plain and simple, I say to myself. *It's time to move on.* You can have your *fuck you* emblem propped in your truck beds, and you can swear with it all you want. *Just keep it from flapping in my face.*

A stretch of uninhabited road follows the bend in the river, running alongside the abandoned railroad tracks, almost to the school—a tiny twenty-second stretch—drags me out of the city by the river's pull, mind floating off somewhere.

Gospel

Just landed at JFK, about to head into Manhattan for the first time in a while. Instead of flagging a cab or jumping into a van, I follow the signs to the Air Train, three stops to the A line, joining a huddle of men and women on the cold and gray platform, wind shuttling in. What about that cold embrace speaks to my bones? What about this congress of strangers?

The whole ride, letting the wider world in, not looking up, just listening to the bodies around me settle into the silence. Only glances allowed, brief encounters with faces. Train car slowly filling. Dipping down into the long, dark tunnel. A young man enters the car and introduces himself.

"I'm not here to bang you or bore you," he sing-songs. "I'm here to sing to you, brothers and sisters."

Of course, no one looks up; nothing spectacular in this scenario. Though the man beside me leans down and opens his stance a notch, he turns his face to hear our singer, nodding as he climbs the verbal steps up onto his soapbox.

"I don't do R&B. Don't do rap."

All I see for now are his red sneakers, his nervous strut back and forth.

"People, I sing gospel."

The train pushes further through Queens. And even though the young man's flock heads into their days wrapped up in headphones and handhelds, I can feel the car tune into the sweet singing. It's all in the eyes. People trying to figure out what exactly is happening, how much effort they will be required to put forth in response. One middle-aged man even gets up and moves further down the car.

"There is no friend like Jesus," the young performer belts.

The congregant beside me nods a fraction. We're approaching a stop. The song is through. There's a moment to ad lib, so a brief bio gets offered up: "I'm only twenty-six. I've banged and boozed. I've seen it all."

My seatmate slips a few coins into the man's hand as he offers up a little fist pump of thank you. A tired-looking trans woman stares at me as I watch the show.

"I've been shot three times."

Someone laughs out loud at the back of the car. This makes our young pastor smile, and he turns to engage the commentary.

I want to give the man a dollar, want to offer up some thanks of my own. But I stop myself, not wanting to make my first overt act in the City be reaching for bills in a tight front pocket. He drifts off to his next stage.

My seatmate gets off at the next stop. The car fills with a new surge, and in the next length of time, I give my thanks by humming quietly in my body, letting in as much as I can, offering praise to this daily gathering of bodies, faces, lives, glances, mute stares. *I'm here to sing*, the young man said. It makes me want to cry. I lower my head instead and fall deeper into my seat, letting the woman beside me settle into my shoulder.

Soon, we'll be under the river, and I'll step out into the great canyons of wind and light. But, for now, here, I will quietly sing into my own breath.

Need Work

When I see the white-haired gentleman standing on the meridian strip holding a cardboard sign, I instinctively reach for spare change. I normally keep dollar bills in one of the dashboard cubbies. *Good luck*, I say. *God bless* usually the answer.

But today no spare bills, no loose quarters. I roll down the window anyway and smile at the man. "Nothing on me today."

The first time he saw me do this, Avery asked me why I bothered to say anything if I didn't have any cash. He's a savvy kid, especially around money.

"Everyone needs encouragement," I said, hearing the sanctimony dripping off the words.

I tried again. "And no one likes to feel invisible."

A nod and Avery was back on his phone.

After a moment, he looked over with a smile: "You do this because it makes you feel better."

On the meridian, the man hasn't moved. He goes on to say, without turning to look at me: "I don't like doing this. My people don't *do* this."

The man bristles with pride and an anger that seems ready to tip into a humiliation he's just as determined to fight off.

I nod, watching a cop drift past a small caravan of homeless men and women.

"At least it's good weather."

It's his turn to nod. The light flips from red to green.

"I've decided this is my last day."

I look at his sign and see he isn't asking, as I assumed, for money.

He glances over once, then turns his gaze off into the distance, readying himself for the next shift of cars.

"I can't do this anymore."

"You'll get there," I say, not sure what I mean by *there*. A light honk from the car behind me and I drive on.

Across the Tracks

Buckle, TN

You're just passing through, sitting alone in the corner finishing your standard diner breakfast—scrambled eggs, bacon, hash browns, toast, coffee. Six, seven farmers are sitting around a cluster of metal tables in this roadside diner's back room. Talk swerves to local gossip. One of the younger guys, cap back on his head, says to no one: "Drivin' up 130 the other night, I near rode up on Larry's truck, the hay bales were hanging so low over the lights. He was so dark it was like he weren't even there."

Another guy chimes in. "He was dark alright, but he was lit up too."

A chuckle percolates out of the old-timer by the door. He sits up in his seat.

"Remember when Larry was with that lady? From up in Nashville—her hand in his wallet all the time?! She got him to dye his hair, and he came in with the whole thing black?"

The men laugh.

"I had to look away to keep from laughing. His whole head, coal black. Sideburns, 'stache, the whole show. Dang near lost it."

You've had enough. You place bills on the check, throw a nod at the kid behind the front counter, and step out into the morning chill as the guy wraps up his story. You must have missed something, for you have no idea what he means when he says: "You can let me off any time." But, as you pass back across the tracks, the whole way to the car, you can hear the men laughing.

Livin' Large at Snapper Jack's

Folly Beach, S.C.

The wind is so persistent up here, the seagulls float above the tables, wings flapping to keep in place before making little dives at tossed tortilla chips. The salt in the air rubs on my skin like liquid sandpaper. The blare of sun infiltrates everything but the darkest sunglasses. I've downed my first gin-and-tonic, served in a plastic cup, two-day-old lime chunks floating in the fast melting ice. There's generic rock-and-roll blaring from the speakers. All the tables are full, the bar now two deep. Everyone's talking or laughing or downing a drink. I don't know a soul. All my people are back at the beach house. I've got a book to crack open, time and thirst for a second drink. I couldn't be happier, couldn't be lonelier.

The crowd here is almost entirely white, middle-aged tourists though one side of the bar seems reserved for locals and employees. There's a younger set inside the majority, mostly couples, and everyone is wearing sunglasses, visors, or hats. Most everyone is tan or sunburnt pink. The ocean lays out in a line, twinned by the horizon line; inside this multi-use activity zone, there are any number of surfers, wind surfers, swimmers, boogie boarders, gulls, planes dragging banners, fishing boats, and pelicans in a periodic line that drift along above the beach houses and pass over our heads like a squadron of slow-motion fighter jets.

Usually when I get away from the group, I take a long walk down the northern end of the island, to where an old lighthouse leans, and the marsh and the tidal flats merge with the ocean. Besides the occasional wedding party, the place is usually relatively empty. People fish, bird-watch, walk along the shoreline, look for shells, or ride beach bikes.

But this afternoon I just want to drink in order to get a buzz—to be above it all for a while and let the wind smooth out excess thoughts and worries. And it's working. What is it about being above the maddening crowd, on a deck, surrounded by strangers with expendable cash that makes me want to drink? At least more than usual. Usually this kind of homogenous scene repels me. I'd happily go elsewhere. Is it that I'm at the beach, on a holiday, and thus free of old habits, opinions, desires? Or maybe I come to a place like this because it's neutral? An Etch-A-Sketch I can doodle on. When done, just shake it up and start again.

Whatever the reason, it unsettles me. It's as if I've walked into a Jimmy-Buffet-drenched Groundhog Day moment, with the pelicans reeling by on a track, and the gulls playing their simple parts to perfection. Even the laughs sound canned. I am happy enough downing a second G&T, watching the bartender shake two martini shakers at once, hands over his head, elbows out, like a bored flamenco dancer.

Maybe it is a need to feel superior to the people sweating it out down below. Or a need to feel like I move in an elite circle, at a remove, invited up to a private party most everyone hears about but can't gain access to. It's not the view; we get the same one back at the beach house. It's not the quality of the booze or the music, for sure, for I have better of both back there. So what is it? Anonymity? Disappearing in a crowd? Witnessing, like an embedded reporter or a spy, the dominant system at its clockwork best, or worst?

I've had my drinks, downed adequate oysters, and now waited for the bill. Everyone has retreated behind sunglasses. All I want now is to be transported out onto that marshy point—to disappear in the wind and let it erase everything.

Pizza

"I'm calling from The Fraud Department."

The woman's voice on the line sounds official enough. Maybe I've been found out.

"We fear someone's using your credit card inappropriately."

Prompted, I give out my vital information.

"Thank you, Mr. Matthews. We need to make sure we are, in fact, speaking with you."

But what if this is not actually the fraud department—a *fraud* fraud department—and I've just handed over everything needed to fleece me?

"How do you decide what recent purchases look suspicious?"

The voice explains it to me, but I don't really follow, not able to stop thinking about this "they" that keeps being referred to. The ones who purchased $200 of airplane model supplies online, then $150 of electronic Walmart products. Who are, just this very minute, ordering from Domino's.

I can't help picturing two teenagers in a suburban, upstairs room, sprawled out in front of the computer, laughing and slapping each other on the back. The pizza guy coming to the door. One peeking at the window across the way where he once saw a girl from his school undressing in front of a mirror.

I want to tell the voice on the phone, *Let 'em get the pizza. They're young and are still growing.*

"Don't worry, we've already cancelled your card. Please hold a moment."

I think back to the previous summer at my parents' place. How, at the end of an afternoon outing, the first big raindrops of an expected storm started to fall. Avery was sitting in the back with a friend, cones in hand. We arrived home just as the downpour came, and the boys scrambled up the long front steps, laughing and shouting.

I stood under the garage roof for a moment as the rain ping-ponged on the tin roof, happy and quiet, watching the storm rumble its way across the sky.

The rasp of the Fraud Lady's voice wakes me out of my reverie. Now she is reading from a script—which would make this hoax quite elaborate and worthy of my respect—but I'm not listening. I am hungry and thinking of ordering a pizza.

Invisible

He looked to be in his mid-sixties: compact build, a designer baseball cap tight on his head, beard close-cropped, clutching a smartphone in his right hand. It was eight in the morning, and the guy was wearing sunglasses!

I thought at first he was talking to himself in a quiet mumble, but he had an earbud in and, judging by the few words I could make out ("stocks," "downside"), he was doing business. The woman behind the register greeted him and rang up his breakfast. He either didn't hear her or just ignored her. I watched on as she visibly bristled.

The man kept talking and, when she told him the amount, drew out a considerable fold of bills, pulling out a crisp five and two singles. All the man's movements were slow, deliberate, controlled. He fingered through his change purse and dropped a quarter on the counter. Still talking. The woman made change. The man took his time replacing his wallet and gathering up his items. Never once did he look at her or stop quietly chatting with his business partner—in Dallas? Hong Kong?

When the man finally stepped out of earshot, I said to the woman, "I don't think he was even here."

She chuckled.

"I try not to take it personally when they talk on the phone. But it's when there are people behind in line that it gets to me."

The woman looked after the man then back at me.

"You're not the only person in the world, you know?"

Falafel 5K

I'd agreed to volunteer for the JCC's annual 5K run. I had been given a street corner to monitor and a strange little red vest to wear. The hand-drawn signs were clear, with arrows leading the runners downhill and through the dogleg onto the home stretch. My spot was shady, smack dab in the middle of the quaint Norwood Park neighborhood, just down the road from the synagogue.

Before the runners started to appear, I had chatted with two couples and introduced myself to an elderly lady and her elderly dog. Soon enough a cop car with flashing lights came around the corner followed by the lead runner, who spit and grunted as he loped past. The next two runners, close behind, were equally preoccupied. The fourth runner, the race's lead woman, yelled out to her son, who was waiting for her on the porch.

He yelled, "Go, Mom!"

"Love you!" she called back as she huffed down the hill. Runner number twelve, also a woman, was running barefoot. The boy had come out from behind the fence to join me on the stone wall.

"What's she protesting, anyway?"

A thick clot of tired-looking 5Kers wheeled into view. "Are we home yet?" one weary runner quipped, his gait stiff and awkward. Another asked me how far there was to go.

"You're close," I told her cheerfully.

"You lie," she hissed.

Claps from the couples on their porches. Then the last walkers and one mom pushing a newborn in a stroller. My brain collaged television footage from the Boston Marathon bombing onto the tranquil scene; I had to blink away the flashing images.

Finally, Avery and his gang strolled into view, chatting and laughing. The trailing cop car inched behind alongside an eighty-year-old man willing himself forward. When this strange little parade floated by (high-fives from the boys!), I gathered up my things, took off the annoying vest, and sauntered all the way to the finish line.

Untouchable

The morning headline blares news of protests and police retaliation. A year has passed since Michael Brown was shot dead, then left in the street. Once again, police are out in their battle gear; protesting citizens getting arrested en masse. It's as if one long curfew has extended to cover the four seasons, and they're back in the same lockdown headlock tailspin. Why can't the police put down their weapons and take off their gear and come into the neighborhoods as peacekeepers? It seems obvious: not until the police force alters its approach and agenda, not until the cops stop shooting first (and shooting to kill), will anything truly change. Can't they just recognize that, acknowledge it?

Easier for me to say, safe here in this suburban Eden, untouched. Untouchable? If so, why do I feel so afraid?

We know ourselves only as
far as we've been tested.
—Wisława Szymborska

Blue

Vievee writes of her recent travels in Barbados. Curtis sends me emails during his six months in Buenos Aires. She's staying in a hotel in the capital and, even though she has friends and colleagues around her and work to do in the day, still she says she is lonely, out of sorts in the midday heat. He, despite having the Spanish and being a seasoned traveler, often finds himself disoriented and confused—in the wrong line, unsure of the social situation he has stumbled into.

Curtis works hard, he writes, "to function inside these states of dislocation and faulty translation." Each day he goes out for a walk, often finding himself in some strange quarter of the city. He notes: "Light, there is so much of it. Even the wind is full of color this morning." When he goes into a shop and talks to the clerk, the guy seems surprised by his Spanish, even though it is impeccable, and pretends not to understand.

This dislocated feeling also holds true for Vievee, for whom everything feels different, "new." She is heartened when she sees herself in some of the people, who have the same gap in their teeth, and appreciates how they look at *her*. She enjoys the fish, the spices. The clean sheets she enters for the afternoon nap. She's having a good time.

Which makes me wonder if "displacement" works better for what I am thinking about here. Or, maybe, I'm really talking about my own experience, thrown in to relief by my friends' travels. That I'm displaced, too, despite having been so place-bound for so long, and so shut-in. Living in a bubble inside a bubble inside a bubble as I do. Maybe it's the state-of-mind part I am thinking of—being *dis*-located as a form of depression or insecurity. Not so much in the wrong location but out-of-place inside oneself.

My anthropologist friend, John, tells a story about being an "idiot dog" when you're out of your element. You don't know the basic things to survive, don't know what to do or how to be, and thus are lost and without bearings. It's a great story I won't tell in full here, but its punch line gets enacted by an aboriginal elder. He's trying to communicate to an anthropologist staying in his village, pointing to the sky to show him where rainwater comes from.

It strikes me that maybe both Vievee and Curtis are feeling lonely; that they are wrapped up in some sort of restless state I can only name "being blue" but that also could be called "feeling alive." Or, again, maybe it's just me. Sitting here on my back porch, living vicariously through them, I feel a brand of sadness that helps me inhabit my body; the kind that comes when you're out in the day—when life overwhelms, a pervasive aloneness. *I'll take this blue feeling and use it to my advantage*, you say under your breath. *Look how good I look in blue.*

Team Player

We're at a soccer tournament down the mountain. I walk up to a pair of soccer dads from our team and say hello. They grunt back *Hey* then wait for me to move on. Their conversation starts back up after only a few steps. Another father turns into his phone as I approach.

Still another dad, at halftime, stressed by our team's dire predicament, shakes his head curtly when I say, "This is no fun." He doesn't want to hear it. In fact, the only man who responds at all nearly jumps when I greet him. Assuming we're on the same team, he asks which boy is mine. I don't have the heart to correct him.

But maybe it's not that cut and dry. The man on the phone makes an effort later; and the dad who shakes his head at me is generally grumpy, and I should have known better to engage him at such a stressful moment. Maybe I am just too sensitive for this crowd. It has been a long drive, it's hot, our team is getting its butt kicked, and maybe I don't know my role, my boundaries. Maybe these men just want to be left alone. Or, maybe, they're just acting like the middle-class American males I deep down expected them to be.

As I walk back to my car, the first two dads approach. They are grinning.

"You missed it."

"Missed what?"

"Man, it was some kind of fall."

It seems that Avery, still in his cleats, slipped on the cement trying to kick the ball and fell straight on his butt. They are both smiling at me. I laugh along, sensing this is my admission ticket, but inside I am quaking.

Neighborly

A neighbor spies us lighting firecrackers down in the gulley. He's scrounging for something in the grass.

"We're lighting fireworks off in our yard at dusk. Come on up. Bring what you got left."

An hour later Avery and I trek up the hill to find a dozen or so adults crowded onto a front yard watching twice as many kids light a variety of roadside fireworks. I've walked up with a beer in one of those beach koozies, surprised to find the whole adult scene booze-free. It makes me feel self-conscious.

Avery is happy, though. He joins a phalanx of neighbor kids and shows off his firecracker stash. The crowd moves to another yard when someone confesses to having illegal fireworks they hope to shoot off their porch. Indeed, a gallery of fireworks burst into the sky, loud bangs and blooms of saturated color streaming momentarily in the sky, drawing the requisite *Oohs* and *Aahhs* from the crowd.

One of my neighbors sees me coming and turns away to avoid me. I don't blame him. Almost every afternoon he walks his three mismatched, cagey canines on the road below our house. My canines have much to say on such pageantry, a flow of invective aimed at the show below: *You suck! You suck! You suck!* Just the other day we met them on the road. Dogs stood around and snarled as leashes formed and reformed as we flashed venomous stares.

Another neighbor approaches—a friendly woman who runs with her friend and waves as she passes me on my dog walk. Her husband and I have gone to a music show together. We jam fingers into our ears and try to chat around the explosions. She tells me about her acting class, then says, politely: "I want to read your novel when it comes out."

"*If* it comes out," I remind her.

Our talk drifts back to fireworks and kids. She introduces me to her father, retired, who writes books and self-publishes. I do my best to extract myself from the conversation without offending the old man.

I share a few passive phrases with my neighbors, though no one is trying too hard to connect. Fine by me. Walking home with a happy Avery, the road dark and wet from a rain, I am glad to have fulfilled my dad duty without anyone losing an eye, without pissing anyone off or making a fool of myself.

Dining Out

Minneapolis, MN

The last night in the city your foursome lucks into a small Ethiopian joint, late. You're happy to grab a seat by the window. The place is full of young men and women, families, older couples. Settling into the scene like bathers letting their bodies down into steaming water. The meal comes, you eat, laughing and conversing, reaching over each other to spoon up more food in your hands. Your waitress comes over, and you stop what you're doing and listen to her describe the meal you are enjoying. Bracelets dance and shimmy on her arms as she speaks. Her smile brings smiles to your faces.

The night before, your group followed a young hostess through an upscale restaurant to the back table—furthest from the door, only a few feet from the waiter station—and stalled there. The place was nearly empty. Was she seating you there because of the differences in your skin color? Was she told to do this by the manager? You asked her for another table, pointing to one in the center of the room. She hesitated, only giving in when your group seated yourselves.

Now, past midnight, two young girls start dancing to the music blasting from the speakers. They are swaying in the aisle for their family and friends. Their dresses shift back and forth against their willowy legs. You watch all of this from the side, catching only glimpses, not wanting to intrude. When the girls stop and everyone starts clapping, you join in. You are so happy. You want the night to go on and on.

War v. Peace

The small movie theater is brimming, half with adults with kids and half with adults with other adults; the cookie-cutout blockbuster rumbles like an elephant barreling down a bowling alley. Ten minutes into the new *Avengers* movie and I am already in trouble.

I've seen enough of these movies with Avery and his buddies to know what I am in for: the strangely thin CGI effects, the video arcade war games, the flat, unfunny banter the superheroes tossed off back and forth on invisible headsets. Why they enjoy this shit, I don't know. I count one laugh from our row, not a single cheer.

And what's with Iron Man's weirdly calm monologues inside that silly armor suit? Like all that hyperkinetic flying about doesn't jostle him an ounce?! I am sick of all this bloodless mayhem, fight scenes cut so fast you can't tell who is doing what to whom. All of it present within the opening scenes, set in predictable motion, the next hour and a half already predetermined. I don't care who they are fighting or why they are fighting. I'm not supposed to. It's just Hollywood talking about itself again.

Hell, the bad guy is an operating system—a rogue computer with a jacked up super-conductor brainstem. And it doesn't take long for the thing to take human form—equal parts Darth Vader, Terminator, and some bored dandy thug. And all of a sudden the team of superheroes (who've been divided and nearly defeated simply by being forced to see their own dreams!) come together as a unit, bonded by the call to duty, and turbocharged back into doing their job. But now they aren't slaughtering the enemy; they are evacuating an entire city. Their love and care is so thick I almost gag. America is suddenly both the avenging *and* the peacekeeping angel. At the same time!

Disgusted, I head out to take a piss, then step outside to check on the state of dusk in the parking lot. Before the accident, at a family movie with Avery, I noticed that the warning under the 'G' rating read *mild peril*. I laughed out loud. That's like saying "just a little death."

What's gotten into me? I used to love this kind of movie. Used to walk out into the night, pumped up and smiling; now it just feels like anesthesia keeping me in this bubble, locking all of us in constant shell shock.

I should go back in, but I stay out long enough to miss a few more important plot points, spared having to connect the numbered dots.

Patience

Two flight attendants take drink orders from the passengers in the seats before you. You are sitting on the aisle in an emergency exit row not far from the first-class partition. A woman is waiting in the aisle across from you; she's returning from the mid-cabin restroom and is blocked by the cart. You see the flight attendant nod to the woman and hold up her finger. A few minutes later, looking up from your book, you are surprised to discover the woman still waiting, now for close to five minutes. The woman in the other aisle seat watches the scene unfold, shaking her head in disgust. The two flight attendants are white women and the waiting passenger black.

At this point, a male flight attendant appears from first class and asks to be let through. This seems a perfect time to let the woman return to her seat. However, the attendants find a way to block her. You watch the woman's face carefully. She remains outwardly calm, but now her arms are crossed at her waist. The woman beside you shakes her head again as the two attendants make sure to avert their gaze. Unable to remain silent, you stand up and approach the woman, touching her lightly on the shoulder.

"I'm sorry," you say. "It's not fair."

She gives you a brief smile and says softly, "I'm used to it. I'm patient."

She turns back to waiting. Meanwhile, and to your astonishment, the lead flight attendant begins serving people in the row *behind* you. The second attendant avoids your gaze again as she takes her time serving her row. The woman bristles with barely concealed anger.

You've had enough. You stand up again, ready to confront the flight attendants. But, seeing you stand, the woman steps up to the back attendant and asks to be let through. She repeats herself. It's at this point that the flight attendant moves the cart back and allows the woman to take her seat. The attendant never apologizes, fails to serve the woman her snack or a complimentary beverage.

A few minutes later, you overhear the woman across the aisle ask her seatmate in halting English, "Does this happen a lot here?"

Close

A quick look of mischief in her eyes. "Who'd you vote for?"

I was getting a six-pack of beer, the obligatory *I Voted* sticker an emblem on my shirt. The young clerk couldn't have been more than seventeen. Tall, thin as a rail, her light-brown skin unblemished, hair plaited perfectly. I said: "Hillary."

"I'd vote for Bernie."

"Yeah, I get that. I almost did, too."

She hovered the six-pack over the scanner. "Then why didn't you?"

I chose my words carefully. "I'm not sure he'll make an *effective* president."

She grinned. "Better than Trump."

"Oh yes, much better."

The man behind me in line shifted his weight from foot to foot, a pinched frown shellacked on his face. I didn't care who heard or how it made them feel. Nor did the young woman, who went on a brief but passionate diatribe about Trump's many deficiencies.

I slid my card and tapped *yes* and *no* as the clerk snapped a green rubber band between her fingers. She said: "That white man is evil."

I was taken aback—not by the sentiment, I wholeheartedly agreed—but by the way the young cashier attached the adjective to the noun. A flash of worry in her eyes as she ripped off the receipt and handed it to me. "Not that you're like that."

I looked her straight in the face. "If that's being white, I don't want to be white."

Gentrified

The history of slavery and its aftermath reveals that
at least some of the nation's cherished green spaces
began as black spaces.
—Elise Lemire, *Black Walden*

After a long day of travel and a night of uneven sleep, I slipped out of Ali's parents' house before everyone gathered for breakfast. I passed down through a young apple orchard and was halfway down the block before I walked past a dilapidated, one-story house—an anomaly on this New England street of fancy, remodeled homes.

I had walked by it dozens of times and never quite noticed the dead elm standing in the heart of its wild field, nor the uneven line of an old stone wall further in, nor the beat-up truck hidden in plain sight beside the dilapidated barn. The reason why no one but the neighbors ever sees this place—and then only to grumble about property values or imagine what they'd do with the land—is that it no longer belongs here, not in this condition, not among all these upsized homes. And I don't usually see it because I am not expecting to find the past plopped squarely inside the shiny present.

Later, over a buffet lunch, I asked about the property. I was told that it was owned by an old man, one of two brothers still alive. He was ill and so didn't come out much anymore.

"The only African-American man," my mother-in-law added, "left in the neighborhood."

My unexpressed thought: *How many lived here in the first place? And how long ago?*

When I pressed for more information, Diane shook her head.

"No one gets to know each other very deeply on this block."

She looked resigned by this fact. And I believed her.

Still, when I looked up the town's census figures online, I discovered that in a town of over 300,000, there were less than 125 black residents. Its most famous black citizen? Cato Freeman, dead now for 165 years.

In *The Color of Law*, Richard Rothstein noted that in one popular history book used in public schools (2012 edition), out of one thousand pages, there was just one sentence on the subject of segregation: "'African Americans found themselves forced into segregation.'" "That's it," Rothstein wrote. "One passive voice sentence. No suggestion of who might have done the forcing or how it was implemented."

The family, the gossip around town went, was expected to sell the property, and another McMansion would rise up in its place. As if it were a foregone conclusion that they would uproot and find a more welcoming place. But why this expectation? Might someone in the family decide to keep the house, fix it up, and start a new family there? They could midwife it even deeper into its wild state. Start a garden. Raise bees. Cut down the dead tree and plant a new one. Fix up the stone wall and talk over it, like Frost would, with the neighbors further up the hill.

I imagined this as I headed out the next morning, again searching out a little solitary time. I resisted the Thoreauvian urge to trespass further into the field. More than likely, though, this place would be gone the next time I came here. And maybe even I won't remember its former presence.

Not a Joke

This morning, as if conjured up from an anxiety dream, one of those mammoth, diesel-powered trucks rolls up behind me. I am walking the dogs, and so lightly pull them onto the embankment to make room. I keep my head down, not liking how close the truck is getting. It drifts by slowly. Though the windows are tinted, I can *feel* the glare of the men I know are inside. The truck keeps inching up the hill, the driver's foot barely on the gas. Then the beast turns around: the driver using the mouth of a side street to pull off his backward "y" pivot. And it comes back down the road, briefly slipping onto the grass a hundred yards ahead before centering back in the road and drifting my way. The leashes taut in my hands.

A few days have passed since Avery tried to tell me an off-color joke he heard, no doubt, in school. I stop him from completing the joke and spend the next half an hour lecturing him on racism and bullying. It has been a year since the Charleston shooting, which still weighs heavy, and I want him to make the connection between a joke and that young man's soulless decision. He knows I am right, but I can see him tuning me out.

The truck pulls up alongside me. Maybe the men are just looking for a place to park. Maybe they're lost or want to talk about my dogs. Maybe not. This time I keep walking. As the car drifts by, I look over with as bland a look as I can muster. The men in the front seat stare right through me. A man in the back seat (it's that big a truck) turns his baseball-capped head and tracks my gradual disappearance. The truck stops again at the bottom of the hill. I pause and wait to see what these men will do next. After a long minute, the truck speeds up and revs around a turn. And, you better believe it, I listen for the low rumble of that diesel-laden truck the whole walk home.

Foul Intake

In the run-up to the election, many things in my life went out, broke, fell apart. My back, for starters. My smartphone, which turned off mid-text. The front doorknob came off in my hand. But it was the heater going kaput that snapped things into focus: nothing like waking to a chilled house to feel the morning's stark news in the bones. Outside, the neighborhood was dim, dark, and dreary. It didn't help that, after months of drought, a rash of forest fires in the Great Smokies National Forest draped Asheville with a tarp of smoke. After a week of the foul intake, everyone started to get lung sick. People walked around with rags held to their mouths, eyes ringed red from the raining ash. As for me, it took a trip to the chiropractor to bring my back online. A few awkward screwdriver turns, and the door was newly knobbed. Heat back on. My phone, well, I just didn't know how to reboot it.

It is not so much that I should have predicted that Americans would elect Donald Trump. It's just that I shouldn't have put it past us.
  —Ta-Nehisi Coates

Improvise

I like to sit in 5 Walnut's back room in the afternoon—a little art gallery—and drink a beer before the place fills up with tourists. I read a book, jot notes down on my pad, or watch the passersby walk first in front of then past the large plate-glass window. Usually it's just me back here. I open the door to let the breeze in, play jazz quietly on my phone.

Today Bobby joins me, plopping down in a nearby chair. He lets me buy him a beer.

Bobby is famous around town for all the restaurants he has washed dishes for. For being such a nice guy. He's one of those sweet loners who everyone likes but, for the most part, keeps to himself. And Bobby seems to like it that way. He has his circle of friends he sees here at 5 Walnut.

Bobby's talkative today, eager, it seems, to reflect on his childhood.

"I tell ya, growing up the way I did in Chicago, it teaches you things."

"Like what?"

He thinks on it a while, sipping down his beer. "That you need to always work hard. And when there's no work, you improvise."

I nod my agreement, not sure Bobby will talk to me in this manner again.

"That's the word," he says. "Improvise."

A moment of silence. He tells me: "I was a crack baby, you know. That's why I walk like this."

He points to his legs. I don't know what to say, so I nod. I think about my once broken legs and those first few years after the accident and feel a small wave of kinship with Bobby, though I know the sympathetic connection only goes so far.

A man walks past, across the street, stumbling and lurching, shouting out to no one.

"It's too early," Bobby comments, "for that boy to be cracked out."

I assume the man is drunk, but looking closer, he seems haunted by ghosts.

"I'm not going out there and play Superman," he says. "That don't get you anything but trouble."

Later, as I get ready to head out, Bobby tells me that, now that we've talked: "We have a thing, you know. We can sit down now and talk to one another."

He takes off his bright yellow cap and rubs his close-cropped head. "Like adults."

Ricochet

North Myrtle Beach, SC

Walking down a long, empty strip running parallel to the beach. The sun sits on your head like an overweight cat. On your left, empty lots; on the right, a row of two- and three-story beach houses, most empty, all tucked behind bushes and narrow sand driveways, garbage bins bungee-corded to railings.

You are carrying a bag of groceries, daydreaming about the day's first gin and tonic, when this low-slung sedan pulls up—you didn't hear it coming—and this asshole kid leans out and shouts in your ear, *Fuck you, faggot!* His sunburnt face is split in half by a Joker smile. The car speeds off. You shout after it, *Fuck you!* and stick up your free hand, middle finger raised high, body thrumming inside a wash of adrenaline.

The car slows down, then stops in the center of the road. Two heads stick out on the passenger side, front and back, blank white faces peering back at you. And for a second you are afraid. What if they U-turn and come back to finish what they started? Or back up fast onto the sidewalk? What if the vitriol thrown at you is more than teen bluster and boredom? Maybe they truly hate gay people.

You put your bag down and step into the road. *Come on*, you wave. *Let's go.*

After a few long seconds, the heads disappear. A beat. Then the car speeds off, honking its horn as it goes: the horn blasts bounce off building faces and ricochet across the road into empty lots.

Jewish

The day after the Orlando shooting—Avery's Bar Mitzvah only hours complete—our extended families are celebrating over at the house. On the lookout for paper plates, I stop by Lin and Linda's place. Retirees up from Florida, they have become the social glue of our little neighborhood. They are sitting in their living room dejectedly, watching television, close to tears. I sit down with them and try to take in the full impact of the reports. So unbelievable, so hard to fathom. Terrorism rolling up and exploding at all our doorsteps.

Avery and his best friends are an interesting group. Among the three, two are Jewish and one born in Jamaica. I worry about Avery and Alex, who also recently had his bar mitzvah. They wear their Stars of David outside their shirts with pride. And what about Phoenix having a brown face in this ultra-white town? What happens when the three of them pile out of a car to grab sodas at some gas station? Will the police hanging out in their squad car have their inner radar turned on? Will they feel inclined to engage, intervene, arrest? And what will happen to these boys inside that arrest?

I sat Avery down the other day to talk about the recent spate of shootings of unarmed black men by the police. And I talked to him about his being Jewish and the threat of anti-Semitism. And I talked to him about being white and about unearned privilege. I was serious so he listened as I let him know that his friend might be treated differently just because of the color of his skin. He understood; I could see him taking it in. But he didn't really know what to expect. I can't remember if I showed him the videos or kept him from them.

Back in front of the television. Victim's relatives stare into the camera, faces caved in with grief and shock. Linda is telling me a story about our neighbor down the street, who keeps making snide remarks about our other neighbors. Something about *those foreigners* moving in.

"He holes up with his German shepherds and guns," she says, "and quietly hates our liberal asses."

Lin adds: "He can't be all that happy with our being gay, either."

Linda snorts a small laugh, turning her attention to the television. I can't stay much longer, unable to take the televised pain. When I walk back to the party, Avery is jumping on the trampoline with two cousins. I have to restrain myself from calling them inside.

Pro Desk

Robert arrives the morning after Trump gets elected. He's ridden his bike all the way across town. Decked out in his racing gear, he minces inside on his cleats, neon bike hooked on his shoulder. "Good day, sir," he says with mock formality.

For a few weeks now Robert's been renovating our kitchen. Today he'll start pulling out the cabinets. Robert's in his early fifties, originally from Grenada but a longtime Brooklyn resident. His partner is the new writing professor at the college. We've started to get to know each other, meeting for dinner in West Asheville at the Jamaican restaurant, hanging out together at a small dinner party. Robert and I like to listen to reggae and King Sunny Ade on the stereo while we work (he renovating, me writing) and end the day on the porch with a puff or two.

Much of our conversation of late has focused around how divided the country is becoming—us against them, black versus white, blue state vs. red. We have watched Trump make his improbable run through the Republican ranks, then, to our minds, steal the presidency from Hillary. We agree that the hostility has become palpable—in social media, of course, but also in the way people drive their cars and in the way folks encounter one another in the grocery store, on the soccer field sideline, along the downtown sidewalks. It's been tense everywhere since the 2008 recession—with all the hatred and barely disguised racism thrown at Obama for his entire two terms—but this feels different, as if Trump has turned the dog whistle into a clarion call.

"You can't let one man, one party, one election rule you, man," Robert tells me at least once a day. Always the same thing: we can't let this horrible situation bring us down.

■ ■ ■

The woman behind the Pro Desk says something to let us know she is a liberal. She looks the part of an old hippy from Vermont, which it turns out she is. Her name is Jackie.

"I'm the only one in the whole store," she confides, showing me the Bernie pin on her apron.

"Good luck with that," I say, sarcastically.

Robert leans in, mock-whispering, "Let's hope Trump don't ruin everything."

Behind us in line, as they have been all week, men and women seem to be speaking in code, whispering about *prizes* and *games won.*

"Ah, you don't like Trump either."

Her look is conspiratorial with a whiff of sarcasm.

Robert looks over at me with eyebrow raised.

I say: "No, not at all. He's the worst of America."

"Obama then?"

She seems unimpressed as she says it.

"A big fan," I reply. "Not perfect, but a classy dude who cares."

When Robert nods in agreement, Jackie joins in.

"Well, we need a change." Then, as punctuation: "Just not Trump."

She pauses for a moment, her face turning serious as she folds the long receipt scroll in half and hands it to me.

"You know what it feels like?" she asks. "*Game on.*"

We nod in agreement.

Robert adds: "There's nothing in us, or around us, that is broken or that can't be fixed. We can't let any sort of bitterness or anger or hatred take over."

"You're right," Jackie says. "The system is broken. Not us."

Robert grabs my arm.

"That's what I've been saying."

Choke Hold by Cop Killed NY Man, Medical Examiner Said

1 Dead as Car Strikes Crowd amid Protests of
White Nationalist Gathering in Charlottesville

9 Killed in Shooting at Black Church
in Charleston

11 Killed in Synagogue Massacre; Suspect Charged with 29 Counts

Orlando Gunman Attacks Gay Night Club, Leaving 50 Dead

Police Shooting of Tamir Rice
is Ruled a Homicide

Death Toll is at 17 and Could Rise in Florida School Shooting

Sandra Bland Threatened With Taser, Police Video Shows

12 Officers Shot at Dallas Protest against Police Shootings

A Burst of Gunfire, a Pause, Then Carnage
in Las Vegas That Would Not Stop

Philando Castile's Last Night: Tacos and Laughs,
Then a Drive

Emergency Declared in Ferguson After Shooting

Respect Yourself

It didn't take me more than a second to type "Yes!" on my phone when a friend wrote he had an extra ticket to the Mavis Staples show that night. Not long after the horrible election results, I needed a little dose of soul.

And Mavis didn't let us down. She talked to the crowd the whole first set about staying positive, not giving up the fight against fascism and intolerance. She reminded us how much her generation had to give up to obtain civil rights, that nothing worth anything comes easy.

By the time her band broke into the Talking Heads's "Slippery People," I'd dropped all my worries and started dancing. For a few minutes I forgot about Trump and what our world was likely to become under his presidency.

A few songs later, an elderly woman standing behind the Mavis counter waved me over.

"Who taught you to dance, son?"

I laughed and shrugged sheepishly as, above us, Mavis owned the stage.

"Well," she said, handing me a bottle of water, "you can come to my party anytime."

Blue Nude

There's a jazz to moving through a day in Manhattan, an openness to improvisation required—stepping into the street, finger raised for the next top-lit taxi—descending into subway tunnels, rushing up to the next car, slipping in before the doors jerk close—side-stepping a crowd of bundled-up construction workers or passing into an impromptu circus scene at the mouth of Union Square or lending an arm to the old woman stuck at the curb, made immobile by the ice. Deep into the last weekend of the Matisse cut-out show at MoMA, the crowd converges in a room and circles the walls filled with playful collage, taking in all the bright colors and whimsical shapes, the flowing lines, moving in and out of each other's sight lines, mumbling *sorry* and *no problem*. I position myself to get some face time with one of the four Blue Nudes—my eye moving back and forth along the figures. Taking a clandestine snap with my phone. Bending down to read about their genesis. Matisse's assistant, Lydia, says, "A small thing, blue on white. That was the start." In the last room, everyone seems high on joy, laughing and nearly dancing with one another. We've been showered with such grace and play, reminded what hard work and perseverance in the face of death can accomplish. Walking out into the winter gray. Finding a bar to rest in, choosing a drink and a few appetizers. Letting our little table get lost in the group babble. Going back through the show together. One of us, an artist himself, shakes his head and says, "He was just an old man in bed with a pair of scissors. I fucking hate the guy."

For Lady V, Who Says She Doesn't See Her Face in Any of My Collages

after Lorna Simpson

When I walk in, an invisible docent stills my breath with a small hand gesture, reaches in, winds up my heart then lets me go—all wobbly spinning—hundreds of small snapshots pinned on the walls in computer code mosaic—vintage pin-ups next to newly-staged copies repeated across the walls—each one a wink. I think, *You've wanted just this exact thing.* I think, *Here are all of your faces, each one of your thousand poses.* Piano jazz seeps out of an adjacent room, elegant, geometric—I dance in its parquet, silent stroll, stutter step. Beauty with plaited braids on bed, knees up. Lady of the Skin in Lamplight, uplifted chin. Sultress reclining sipping a martini. Sexpot draped over a sedan, circa 1957. *Ebony* pin-up—hair piled, legs slightly spread—on day bed. I think, *This is what you need, a room like this to walk into for every time you forget.* I think, *This is what you need to remind you you are beautiful.* This gallery of women, just for you, ready and willing, each pose a possibility, framing so—just so—you can look straight into all your own faces.

Walking Lubbock

It's inevitable. Whenever Curtis and I get together, we go out for a long ramble. As we do this lovely morning, sauntering through Downtown Lubbock. It is early fall and unseasonably cool; it even rained a little. We wear light pants, T-shirts, sneakers, both hefting backpacks filled with books and extra gear. *Saunterers.*

It is only a few suburban blocks to the Texas Tech campus, Curtis's standard route to work. A trio of barky dogs follow along a long fence, tails wagging, then wait with us until we cross the eight-lane boulevard, watching as we sidestep the SUVs and the giant puddles caused by flash flooding.

We have been talking about the state of affairs in Lubbock, in Texas, in the country. Trying not to fall into despair. I worry aloud that our world has moved "beyond repair." Curtis pushes back on the thought. *Is anything really ever* beyond *repair?* I try to explain myself. *I mean, why even try to repair something so broken?* We bat the idea around. Maybe it's not about systemic failure—as in, *That car is dead, it's beyond repair*—but, instead, about something transformational—as in, *We need to move* beyond *repair.* Not trying to *fix* something but overhauling the whole system. Throwing everything out and starting again.

As we pass out of the walking paths and student buildings and parking lots, we move into a new kind of grid. Downtown Lubbock feels bombed out, abandoned. Whole blocks of empty warehouses, old brick buildings with boarded-up windows. I joke about it being like an episode of *The Walking Dead*.

Curtis sticks up for his adopted city. "It's more complicated than that. You're reducing the place."

Right on cue, we come upon a pair of well-dressed men speaking Spanish strolling down the middle of the street. They give us a polite nod as they pass.

Further down the block, men sprawl out in a rough semi-circle around a homeless shelter, chatting and chilling. Another turn and we are heading through campus housing. Our talk has turned to the upcoming break, and the time he and Idoia will spend in Spain. I admit my jealousy of their freedom, their adventurous life—a way of being that has all but vanished for me post-accident. (This trip to Lubbock one attempt to alter that!)

It takes us a moment to realize that we are walking too close behind a woman. We slow our pace, allowing her the space to get to her car without the potential menace of our presence. Soon we are crossing back over the boulevard jammed with cars that don't make room for two guys on foot. Somebody honks. The puddles have evaporated. The dry heat rises up off the ground in an invisible waft. And the dogs come running.

Poet

Ever since the storm hit, we've been out of power. Haven't washed for three days, more than a little sleep-deprived, nerves frayed, entirely ravenous. Avery has holed himself up in his bedroom, windows open despite the mosquitoes. Ali stays out on the porch, wrapped up in the hammock chair. Like a nurse shark, I float back and forth, in and out, room to room. For all the above, this invite to brunch feels like a thrown lifeline. A much-needed respite from ourselves during this rerun episode of Disaster Light.

And so, over a steaming dish of scrambled eggs, after hearing our sob story, a woman whose husband is a poet asks: "Can you even change a light bulb?" She's joking, kind of. I've played this brand of straight man before. However, also being a poet, I'm light on my verbal feet.

"No, but I can change it into something else."

Not a foot in a trap,
but a foot in a trap and
the snow getting deeper.
—Vievee Francis

Boxes

I'm in a group of writers sitting around a table in a hotel in Chapel Hill, wine and sparkling water at hand. The *Odyssey* has come up, and someone says something about the wandering hero. I quip, "Maybe that rock wasn't such a hard place."

The elder at the table chimes in: "There's a post-colonial read on Circe, you know. Odysseus gets waylaid there, sure, but he's so sick and tired of the empire and is having way too much fun in the Islands to ever want to leave."

He has a way of laughing that makes everyone else smile—a kind of lilting, manic rush of *ha ha ha* with his eyes squeezed shut.

Another writer looks up at the ceiling, frowning. The speaker over her head has been broadcasting moody violin music nonstop. "There hasn't been a major chord all night."

Our first course has arrived. The hummus is literally steaming it's so hot.

The elder tells our end of the table that he hates how black writers are always being boxed in.

"Editors only approach me when it's about race. Never about love or domestic life. Just race. It's maddening."

I ask him if he thinks this is true outside of Britain.

"Even worse," he says, laughing.

Between bites, I wonder aloud: "Maybe you need to write in some other genre, like a mystery novel or something, to get them to stop stereotyping you."

He shakes his head. "Then they will just box me inside the genre."

He starts laughing again. He puts his hand on my arm. When he opens his eyes, they are animated by a distinct sadness.

"I am going to make you an honorary black man for a moment, if you don't mind."

I nod enthusiastically.

"And so, as an honorary black man, I'd ask you to imagine being shot by the police and falling dead to the pavement. Imagine the cops leaving your body there for three hours in the baking sun just to make sure everyone knows they don't give a shit about any of you, either."

I lean in.

"Now imagine it again, but this time, and just as your body falls forward, you flip out into space and land on your feet in the future."

I fall back against the booth seat as the elder smiles into his whiskey.

My hotel is a short couple of blocks down the road. The night is warm like pond water, with patches of cool and breeze. A faulty streetlight sputters. A car goes by, bass thumping. "Get Low," by Lil Jon & the Eastside Boyz, blasts through the open windows.

The song chimes in my head as I walk. On the corner outside the hotel, before I have time to react, a woman rises from a bus stop bench and grabs me by the hand.

"Hey, get me a room up in there," she says. The man with her stays silent, stock-still as if sitting for a portrait. "That's where you come from, right?"

High Line

"You won't recognize Chelsea," my aunt Susan says slyly as I head out.

And now I am striding up Broadway on a clear spring day, bound for the High Line; and, indeed, as I turn on the appropriate corner, left toward the river, I nearly fall back against a brick wall, hit by a full force gust of glitz and glamor. I am entirely taken off guard by this old neighborhood's newly minted, ultra-hip status.

And all of a sudden, beautiful, well-dressed couples with large name-brand bags hanging from their shoulders are strolling along the sidewalks, crossing crisply into traffic, cell phones stapled to their ears, ducking suavely into fancy clothing stores. Glossy bistros on every corner with large plate-glass windows showcasing more attractive, young couples alongside trendy flower vases and flashy bottles of booze. Elegant older women mince their toy poodles alongside buff, middle-aged men who are being walked by their oversized designer dogs.

And, without consciously being aware of it, I have acquired a new bounce in *my* step. My back has straightened, a hand passed briefly through my hair. Inexplicably, I feel healthier, wealthier, happier, sexier. And I walk this way, buoyed by the scene, in and among the movie-set grandeur, up onto the High Line itself—dancing inside the moving sidewalk of bodies, sidestepping the selfie-snapping hoards—then back down the old elevated steps some blocks later, where I turn another corner and the boulevard drops back to standard Manhattan drab and everyone wears their business-as-usual uniforms—carrying plastic CVS bags and waiting solemnly for the bus alongside homeless men and women huddled together inside doorways, a lone coffee cup out on the sidewalk whispering for loose change.

And I, too, return to my daily self—stiff in the knee, slight headache, in need of a drink or a cup of coffee or a nap—and the whole walk through Chelsea all of a sudden seems like a dream, some demented fantasy my brain has created to counter all the negative tapes that so often run through it, letting grief and fear seep out inside every loop.

Welcome

He's been working at the corner gas station for over a year now, mostly afternoon shifts, sometimes early in the morning, and every day I come in, every time, he smiles and jokes with me and asks Avery questions. He wears his hair long, down to his shoulders, and so he looks like some sort of hippy Bodhisattva in a garish, yellow and red uniform.

Back in the car, Avery says, "He's friendly."

I nod my head in agreement. "Yes, he is."

When I come in next, alone, the man asks again after Avery.

"What sport?"

When I tell him that Avery plays soccer, his smile widens. He mouths *football*.

"What is your name?" I ask.

"Arjun."

"Mine is Sebastian."

We shake hands formally. He gives a slight bow.

The next morning he is positively beaming. I ask, "Something new?"

"Oh, yes," he says, tossing his hands in the air. "My family arrived today."

I smile back, genuinely happy for his man. "From where?"

"Northern India," he says, ringing up my usual items. "A small village you will not know of."

"That's good," I say. "Good to have them with you. Especially now."

He nods his head vigorously.

"Trump," he says.

"Just be careful, please."

He rings me up and hands me the bag. "Will they be here long?"

I am hoping he'll say, *From now on*.

"Oh, yes," he says again. "They will be here for two months."

"I am so happy for you." I shake his hand, and he takes mine in both of his.

"It is a good day to be alive," he says.

When I come back a few days later, Arjun introduces me to his wife and son. They are shy and keep their distance. I lay out my hand for a low five. The boy, who must be eight years old, slaps my hand dutifully.

"Welcome," I say. "Welcome."

It takes me some time to return to the store. I buy my gas early in the morning, or fill up on the road, but weeks go by. I have forgotten about my new friend. There he is, behind the counter, in the usual spot, but no big smile today. A small one appears as I approach the counter, wry, a little hangdog.

"You've been away," he says.

"Yes, that's true. I've been busy." I think, *I am that asshole.*

"How are you, Arjun?"

He shrugs. Then I remember. "Your family, have they gone home?"

"Yes, yes," he says, "they have."

"You must miss them."

"Oh, I do."

He looks away as he hands me the bag. I stand there for a moment. He looks back at me. "After they're gone, I cry for two days."

Notes from Vegas Strip

. . . a land of canned music seeping nostalgically out of every bush. Young women waiting to accompany you in a photo, naked but for pasties, a pair of panties, and a set of bunny ears. A garrulous Elvis impersonator riding around drunk in a scooter cart and insulting passers-by. Earnest men dressed all in black broadcasting the word of Jesus on street corners. Yellow minis, giant hair, and his-and-her T-shirts announcing "King" and "Queen." Billboards like movie screens. The glitter and glare glancing across glass buildings back-dropped by sure-bet blue. Overweight adults lugging flagons of florescent Mardi Gras-style Hurricanes. Freshly washed cars passing dignified under a giant, looping rollercoaster. Eager and desperate young men passing out fliers with signature flair. A stormtrooper next to a Ninja Turtle next to a Transformer next to a man sleeping on the sidewalk, his cardboard sign smudged and illegible. A single, dancing blue M&M. And the grimy old man in the bright orange T-shirt announcing GIRLS, GIRLS, GIRLS . . .

Manager

I am in the lumber section with Robert. He's asking the wood guy about their oak selection. He needs a decent stack of five-by-eight boards. The guy turns to me and starts to answer. I take a half step back and point at Robert. Meaning: *talk to him*. The guy's eyes open a notch and he does just that: he turns to Robert and answers his question. He walks us to the oak before hustling off.

Robert often jokes that I am his project manager, which I kind of am, but only if that means I help him haul supplies to and from the car and pull out the credit card at the Home Depot Pro Desk checkout line. One morning the following week he asks me if I remember the encounter with the guy in the wood department. I nod before he's even finished.

"Oh yeah," I say.

"It happens to us all the time," he says.

"I get it," I say.

He means *black folks* and *white guy*. He means worker and boss. He means, despite my best intentions, that I cannot possibly *get* it.

Wild

for C.

You talk to me about wanting to get higher then higher, climbing up out of the tourist realm, *ahead of the wave*, up early to find the elusive summit. Machu Picchu—the first world's collective wet dream of spiritual sanctuary. *We were there*, you say, ghosting the Lubbock streets as I trek down into a familiar forest, dogs out ahead on the trail. Two friends back in cell phone touch. *We were travelling like we did as kids*, you say. I am only mildly jealous. I can picture you in shorts and T-shirts, tipped forward by top-heavy packs, sweaty and sore, moving upstream inside tourism's mundane turbulence; then dropping your load in the windowless hostel before falling into sleep like water dropped into a glass. But aren't you also out in the wilds as you talk to me, tracing routes onto those high desert streets? And aren't I, too, a little wild, breaking the slender spider webs along the Asylum Trail, the first biped to pass down this trail since nightfall?

X Marks the Spot

After a few minutes on this dusty back road, we spot a line of trucks parked in the ditch and know we've found our place. The building looks like every shack-at-the-end-of-the-road cliché. Its wooden sign proclaims *Line of Fire* inside a gun sight.

We climb out of the car and stretch; the boys join the loose group of men walking around toting paint guns, masks still on. With the faux-army costumes and overall camouflage aesthetic, it feels like a militia in training, or an open call for some warped reality TV show. Outside the front entrance there's a worn and torn American flag drooping from a rusted flagpole. (At least it's not a Confederate flag.) The ground is strewn with flattened bursts of green, yellow, and red paint.

We step inside to sign in, then wait in line for fifteen minutes. Turns out we're in the wrong line, so we take a low-ceilinged trek down into the "retail" section where we sign consent forms—each of us signing our names in at least six places—and pay the middle-aged lady who, gauging from her twangy banter, has just come from a paintball tourney.

It's hot. Everyone is sweating profusely, overdressed for the sport. (I am told later: "It's so the paint bullets don't hurt as much when they hit your body and don't explode.") No one's talking but the lady at the counter. The owner (her husband?) is busy restoring a paint gun, randomly shooting bursts of loud blanks machine-gun fashion into the ceiling.

The boys are nervous; they're the only teens at the place—(Avery grumbles "Fucking professionals" as three faux commandos stroll past)—but seem game and ready to go to war.

■ ■ ■

The week before, I am sitting with my friend Mc at a local bakery. We are sharing stories of the recent culture wars here in Trumpland. I've just told him my "white men in trucks" story.

In turn, Mc tells me about this local fly-fishing guide who meets him in a parking lot somewhere in Mills Valley; how the guide takes him to four spots, one after the other, all "dead," barren of fish. Mc knows what's going on but keeps it to himself. The guide doesn't say a word, either, except to dole out negative feedback.

Guide: "You must be doing something real wrong."

Mc: "I must be doing four or five things wrong."

Later, at yet another spot with no chance for fish, the guide asks: "You from around here?"

Mc: "No. I live in Asheville."

Finally, at end of day, as he takes Mc's money, the guy sneers: "Thank you, Mr. Obama."

As Mc drives off, he realizes that the guy spied his bumper sticker when they first rendezvoused. Which is why the guide has jerked him around, brought him to bullshit spots, taken his money, and wasted his time—all because of that sticker.

Mc: "I thought about going to the place and telling them about this guy. To ask for my money back. But I decided not to."

Me: "Why?"

Mc: "He probably has a family to feed."

The guy behind the equipment counter is wearing a yellow ref shirt on top of his black jeans and black T-shirt. He runs off a five-minute set of rules to the blank-faced boys. They can't do this, or shoot this way, or move this obstacle. If their mask slips off, they must immediately drop into a fetal position. They cannot pick up any dropped paint balls and reload the gun's hopper for it will gob up the works. Wrapping up, he tells them that if they shoot a rat out on the field, they will earn a free bag of paintball pellets. "Free!" he reiterates. The boys' eyes light up.

"I hate this scene," I admit as we walk over to the picnic tables. The boys load up their guns. Ruben asks, "You hate rednecks?"

The group snickers.

"No, that's not it. I've lived in backwoods New Hampshire. I know this. People are people. It's just the whole gun thing, the war games."

The boys don't seem convinced. They join the line out back, the next battle about to begin. And I wonder if the boys might be right. Not hate. Not fear. But maybe a little liberal disgust. I can't help seeing (or imagining) the Trump racism and xenophobia hiding behind those masks. Can't help but read white power in their camaraderie, can't help but feel a quiet dismissiveness emanating from the older men as they take in my yuppie attire.

As soon as the boys disappear into the camouflaged netting, I get back in the car, pull out of the little gulley, execute my best three-point Y-turn, and hightail it to the Sierra Nevada brewery down the road.

King

Oxford, UK

The pub is cozy and quiet. Two elderly professors—visiting faculty, in Oxford for a conference—lounge in the corner, up late to savor a whiskey before bed. A young British couple sits on a nearby couch drinking ale, quietly eavesdropping. Eventually, the young woman leans in and asks the pair if they are from America. The couple teaches American history in their local high school—the Civil War and civil rights, in particular. They've been listening in carefully, aware from the level of conversation that the American professors are scholars at the top of their fields. That they are African-American only makes it better.

The couple moves forward in their seats, eyes widening to the opportunity before them, and ask politely if they can posit a question about Martin Luther King Jr. and whether he was the *central* figure in the Civil Rights movement. One of the professors shakes his head with a tired smile and leans closer.

"Can we take notes?" the young woman asks, only half joking. She knows it doesn't get better than this.

And the professor explains that MLK, at first, was a reluctant leader, and that, when looking at movements in history, you must figure out who stood beside the main figure, looking first to the left (Ralph Abernathy) then to the right (Coretta Scott King), and then you had to look back behind these three representative figures (John Lewis) and learn just how they came to stand in their respective places and just what transpired to bring them to those spots—the who, the how, the why, the what. The bartender announces last call and starts collecting glasses.

When I head up to my room, the young couple is still earnestly asking their questions, and the two professors are still answering them, the quartet of faces close together in the candlelight.

No Trespassing

The Dawsons have reserved a point, replete with fire pit and picnic tables. Your son's league soccer team is meeting at Biltmore Lake to celebrate the end of a long season. Two sturdy ducks with red masks parole the area like boardwalk thugs. A loose circle of parents drink beer. You watch as Bob stacks wood for the bonfire. *Oh, hell*, you think, *I better help Bob.*

But as you approach, you realize it's not Bob but some lake staffer filling the woodbin. You keep walking, pretending you didn't make the mistake. He pretends, too.

This is a wealthy community—WASPy elite, country club, retiree, golf crowd wealthy. The wood the young man has delivered is perfectly cut for the pot. The lawns trimmed to fairway length. You hate these kinds of places. And, despite yourself, you feel at ease in them. On the surface, you fit in. Inside, you are roiling. These are your people's people, not yours.

Now you're approaching the shoreline, which is evenly populated with huge lake houses. There is a trail, "for members only."

I'm with the Dawsons, you'll say, though they don't live here. *They've put me up in their guest quarters.*

The dusk light, the low seventies weather, the steady breeze—all of it feels preordered by the board. You walk until you're out of sight, just you and the roughneck ducks, the rustling trees. Trespass until you feel like turning back.

No one will know you were here.

Car & Driver

Before the car accident, I used to dream often of driving on a two-lane highway—one of those small, curvy ones on the West Coast, with California cliffs dropping down to the ocean—and in the dream I'd get to the point where I lost track of the automobile and was steering from somewhere behind—for the dream had separated car from driver—so now I was unable to see where the car was actually going; and I'd have to steer blind, so to speak, guessing where the car would bank for the turn or when it would pass another car. In these dreams I would often pull off the road, a night traveler stepping out of his car in some lonely gas station, draw in a few deep breaths and stretch out my back before folding back into the car and driving on.

I don't have that dream much anymore. But I remember it as an exhilarating and anxious feeling, a kind of fuck-it-I'll-play-it-by-feel experience. Why not simply let go—a parent behind his child letting go of the bike—and see where the small craft ends up?

What did he just
say? Did she really
just say that? Did I
hear what I think
I heard? Did that
just come out of
my mouth, his mouth,
your mouth?
—Claudia Rankine

Game On

. . . at the Montreal airport

"He is just a stupid, mean man. I feel no empathy for him."

I'm hovering at the mouth of the bar next to the baggage claim. It's late, the place near closing. The woman at the bar is either ranting at the image of Trump on the flat screen or just someone she knows. Stalled by the wall-mounted television in the corner, I check on the Cavs-Warriors game. Game five of the Finals. It's close. *What the hell.* I order a beer and sit down for what remains of the fourth quarter.

When the bartender comes over to deliver the pint, I hear the rustle of a man standing a little bit behind me; he's leaning lightly against a mirrored column. I motion to him in mock gesture, miming a body moving out of the way. *Am I blocking your view of the game? No, no,* he waves, flashing a smile. *You're fine. Stay where you are.*

A few minutes later, he is standing at my side, watching the game, arms around his chest like mine around mine.

Mustafa lives in the city and works in the business sector in some way. He is originally from Kenya, he tells me. He's waiting to pick up his father, who is flying in from his home country. Mustafa grew up playing basketball, still plays pick-up with his friends in a local gym. He's about six feet, maybe an inch shorter.

I ask Mustafa more about his family, but he skirts the issue. He is curious if I have children, then if my son also plays hoops. I describe our one-on-one games in the driveway. How I always talk smack. *You can't teach height! You're slow, old man,* the inevitable comeback.

"I was a small forward in a third-rate point guard's body," I say.

Mustafa smiles distractedly.

"Shooting guard," he says with pride, pointing briefly to his chest before quickly looking back to the game.

My guess, he's in his mid-thirties. Mustafa turns his attention back to the game.

"Which team you rooting for?"

He shrugs with a mischievous smile. "Neither."

I give him a look that asks for more.

"I just want to see LeBron against Durant. I'm not rooting for any team to win. You?"

I confess my affection for the Dubs and for Steph's wizardry.

"Though, actually, if the Cavs win tonight, I'll be rooting for it to go seven."

Mustafa nods his agreement.

And it seems as if the Cavs might do just that. The game's coming down to the wire, and LeBron seems to have everything in control. Five minutes left and the Cavs are up by a bunch. But, as we both know, as everyone watching the game around the world knows, no lead and no amount of time left, no matter how brief, is safe when you're playing the Dubs.

With about three minutes to go, Mustafa and I are joined by four African men, all dressed in airport uniforms. They are speaking in French to Mustafa while acknowledging me in brief spurts of English. Now we're all silent. Are the Cavaliers really going to choke?

I ask Mustafa, *sotto voce*, "Can the Cavs make this a series?"

Mustafa whispers, "I hope so."

Now the game is inexplicably close. Hushed silence. Korver misses an open three; Durant trots the ball over the centerline and rises up over LeBron, drilling his own. All of a sudden the Dubs are winning. Kyrie takes too much time off the clock, turns it over. Curry hits another three. Game over.

Our group disperses quickly. A soul shake with Mustafa and I am out the shudder close of the automatic doors. I spy a cabbie rising off his spotless sedan, dropping his cigarette under his heel.

Who gives a flying fuck about Trump, anyway?

White Dad Shoes

The hip Italian sneakers purchased recently in Montreal have become, in the minds of fourteen-year-old Avery and his best friend, "White Dad" shoes. Avery's latest roasting insult, "You're such a White Dad."

It's not enough that friends keep complimenting me on my *cool shoes*. I have been nailed. I try to tease back by calling the boys *White Dad*.

Phoenix: "I can't be White Dad, I'm black."

Me: "But you're *acting* like a White Dad."

They shake their heads and walk upstairs.

I lather on sunscreen before we go tubing, and it gets stuck in my beard.

Avery: "You look like a demon with your red eyes and that sunscreen on your face."

I moan at him like a ghoul and chase him into the water. Later, he comes out of his room with a complete mask of sunscreen. The boys explode in laughter at his parade of whiteface.

On the way to the movies, I bring it up again. "I am one of the least 'white' White Dads you know."

The boys look at each other with deadpan stares, then return to their games. That's just what a White Dad *would* say.

I pump up the volume on Stevie Wonder's "Boogie On, Reggae Woman."

Stuck in Stowe

Step out of the rental car in this leisure-class ski-town and you get engulfed in a whiteout of J. Crew WASPiness—pushed along the winter sidewalk from boutique to boutique, pausing only to ruffle the head of another catalog Labrador.

The putt-putt place just up the road describes itself as "golf in miniature." The café across the street informs, on a nicely penned sign, just exactly where they get their milk—also just up the road—and from which cows; and the condominium par-course has signs tacked up on top of the exercise instructions urging one to "Always be Humble" and "Set Goals."

The women are all as thin as ski poles; the men walk around like hologram ads for snowboards. All the children seem hand-delivered by Amazon Prime, spilled from their boxes preformed, unleashed onto the golf-green-sized lawn. *Woo-hoo, we're havin' ice cream!* (Though you know it's gonna be gelato.) Whiteness in this town is like a ski pass from three years ago adorning the bottom of a ski jacket. Privilege is just another snow machine.

Get the picture? Now throw yourself in. You've just bought a blue fleece from a clerk who sneers as you slip it on; she lives down the road in Johnson and holds down three jobs and she's seen enough white-haired white guys like you to make a grown woman cry. You slide into this drawing like Waldo. You're so visually correct for this scene you are virtually invisible.

But not quite. There you are in the restaurant window—farm-to-table!—looking blandly handsome, bored, a bit put-upon. *Go home*, you tell yourself. *You're done here.* But there's no *home* to retreat to.

Fence

This, my white friends, is privilege. Even in our most activist
moments, we don a cause like a fashionable hat, briefly, until
we exhaust our emotional reserves.
—Clinton J. Moyer, *Huffington Post*

There's a large Confederate flag hanging on a building outside of town. All day, talk has been of the recent rally in Charlottesville. It's not hard to draw a line back to the Holocaust.

Our friend, Yael, quotes a popular phrase among Israelis: "We were like sheep going to slaughter." She uses it as a crowbar to pry open a tentative argument for resistance.

Someone asks, "Would you stand by and just let them come into your town? Let Trump ruin everything?"

No one answers.

I have been engaging with friends all week, trying to unfreeze my emotions around the latest slate of shootings. It took an op-ed piece in the Huff Post to wake me up. The final crack in the ice already cracking. I've heard it before, thought it before, but something about this man's direct call for whites to get out of their comfortable chairs got to me. Maybe it's how he calls us out for "when it's convenient" activism.

The ice started to melt earlier the week before, while watching *Free State of Jones*, then again when talking with Ali after the movie (in our "cushy cloud of isolation"). There in front of us were brave and activated individuals, white and black, fighting side by side, not giving up, not giving in. It was like watching a Hollywood trope for the Black Lives Matter movement or, at least, a history lesson on what is possible. I felt the same way watching *Selma*. Movie as wake-up call. *Act! Do Something!*

At the recent downtown vigil, two different factions ended up squabbling with one another. I watched an elderly woman in a rainbow shirt, without a megaphone, as she tried to shut down a tight knot of protestors (Antifa?) as they shouted "Cops Equal Klan!"

"We need to come together in peace," the peace activist shouted. The dozen or more radicals got louder and waved their handmade signs at the cars drifting by (some honking encouragement, others revving their engines in passive-aggressive hostility).

The rainbow activist cried out that it was "evil" for the group to try to out-shout hers. It seemed to me, standing back by the fence, straight out from where the speakers were situated, that the faction for "peace" and "love" saw themselves as the event host, and that the folks for "rage" and "revenge" were off to the side. I heard later that they were co-hosting the event.

Now a few of the peace-and-lovers were trying to get us "peaceable folk" to stand in front of the angry activists, so "they don't become the face of why we're here." I refused to budge. Let them have their anger and their fingers raised to the cops. Let them choose rage over peace. In my mind, the two go hand in hand. And why shouldn't we let the world see these two conflicting—balancing?—energies animating our faces. Let the cops filming the whole thing understand we have come to this point. MLK and Malcolm X once again on different sides of the same fence.

Line

My friend in the city warns me, "There's always a line. But it's worth the wait." I trust his taste in breakfast joints and don't mind waiting. During my walk down from midtown, I pass half a dozen churches; on every corner just across from the church, homeless men and women camp, signs out and paper cups in hand. No cash, I keep walking. It's starting to get cold.

I arrive on First and Broadway about twenty minutes early, happy to follow the descending street address numbers down through the brightening swath of morning sun. There's a line of people across the street. It's bright, and my eyesight is particularly poor at mid-range, so it takes a few steps to realize that these men and women are waiting for a soup kitchen to open.

I walk on. Soon enough I spot the line for the breakfast place. Even half blind, the difference is clear. A small clutch of hipsters in wool hats and down coats lingers outside the door, chatting, moving their feet to stay warm. One of the men has pulled out juggling balls and has started a rough parody of juggling. Everyone else peers down at their phone screens. One woman blows softly across her nose ring. I reread the restaurant's menu.

A few minutes before ten, my friend shows up. When the door opens, I file in with the growing crowd, led to one of the small tables in the back. As we pick up our menus, happy to be in from the cold, coffee tipped into our mugs, I'm, all of a sudden, ravenous.

Drift

The elderly man brushed us aside with a harsh hand gesture. *Go, go*, he was saying. *Get out of my sight.* I'd been late to see him and his white-haired partner crossing the intersection and so had stopped short. I'd gestured them on, apologetically. He did it again—a brusque response commanding us to drive on through. I laughed. It was as if I were a servant who had made a predictable mistake.

A poet, now dead, who lived well up in these Appalachian Mountains, once told me that the super rich don't want you to notice their presence, but they can't help marking their territory. *You know they're really rich when their driveway gets marked by a single, mammoth river stone.*

We ended up at a burrito joint on the edge of downtown. It was empty when we got there, but, soon after the noontime bell, it began to fill up. All of a sudden, in a town seemingly made up entirely of preppy, elderly whites, we were surrounded by Latinos, blacks, working-class whites, and teens. "We've come to the right place," I said to Ali, who smiled in agreement. What exactly I meant, I am not sure. More laid-back? More skin tones? Less *rich*?

I watched as a pair of twenty-somethings wrestled the floor mats out the back door. They were laughing at each other as they struggled, kicking at each other's feet to make the task more difficult. Stopping to share hits off a vape pen. As we were heading for our car, the couple from the intersection stepped out of a tony dress store. The woman saw that it was raining—a light splatter of thick drops—and cursed her luck. "We don't have our umbrella," she lamented.

Code

When I walk up, the two young Best Buy clerks are standing face to face at the checkout counter, talking about getting together after work. They are white, clean-cut, only a few years older than Avery.

"You could come by after eight," one says to the other.

"Okay."

The guy in the aisle glances in my direction, then steps out of the way. As his friend behind the counter rings up the single ream of paper, the box of ink cartridges, the dude starts to banter.

"The Second was when it was done, right?"

"Yes," says the other, finishing the phrase: "Not the Fourth. The Fourth was when it was *ratified*."

They nod in unison, grinning. It seems they are putting on a show just for me.

"A good day."

"A good day indeed."

I can't help it. It's late June.

"History nerds?"

The guy behind the counter smiles, about to nod his head. The other guy leans back in, a menacing gloss to his smile: "No, I just love *my* country."

I'm not buying it. It's only been a half-year since the Parkland shooting. This guy is cloaking hate under a flag. I collect my things and, before heading for the door—and against Ali's sage advice to refrain from engaging in such situations—wag a finger at the young man.

"If you love your country, you should know *its* history."

I get a surprised look in return, then a glare, which I meet with a cold, professorial stare. I want to say something about *We the people* but know it would only fall on deaf ears. So I listen to the voice in my head and head for the door, my step picking up only slightly as I approach the car.

Heart of Sol Legare

First the young man with the bright smile working at the T-shirt shop; then the young woman returning my greeting at the hotel's café counter; then the old fisher couple on the bridge angling for red snapper and flounder. The woman smiles: *We'll be out here all day.* Locals, yes, but also my first, and so far only, interactions with anyone who isn't white all week. Otherwise, it's been a constant, friendly but distant presence of other white people on vacation. Maybe a small nod back or a smile (often created by a playful dog or a runaway beach ball), but, most of the time, it has been all mutually agreed upon parallel play.

This changes when my parents, out on a birding adventure, stumble upon the Island Breeze Café, far down an old dirt road. A local man let them know the "the little Gullah place" would be open later that evening and that they should come back and try out the food. And indeed we do, happy to drive up to this low-country joint nestled at the far point of a hidden cove—a stone's throw from Folly Beach but decades away, too. *Hot damn, how'd we end up here?*

It's early evening. We pass a sign that says *Mosquito Island*. We've driven by what appears to be an old, renovated barn and a family picnicking nearby under palm trees. The houses scattered around are mostly one-story, some neat and tidy, others ramshackle. The restaurant has a screened-in porch. There's a bar inside with a pool table and a small square of dance floor; the waitresses serve bright neon drinks alongside Red Stripes in squat brown bottles.

My mom has gotten the idea the place is strictly BYOB, so she has brought wine and beer in bags. I quickly shuttle them back to the car, stashing them behind the back tire. There's a table of locals taking their time with their seafood platters. Our group of eight gets accommodated easy enough by dragging three tables together. (The place is so small we constitute a rush.)

After a few minutes, a woman in her thirties walks over. She introduces herself as Giovanna. She is wearing a colorful dress, her hair in braids. She starts to tell us about Gullah culture and, in her words, gives us "an oral history lesson." Giovanna tells us this place is called "Sol Legare." I can't remember now, but the name had something to do with the original settlers, freed slaves who came to Mosquito Island in the late 1800s.

She lets us know about the recently opened nightclub just a little further down the point. She's part owner of the Def Club, proud of the young hip-hop scene growing there.

"Yeah, our little joint gets a little wild at night."

Ali asks about the renovated building we passed on the way in.

"It was a meeting hall."

She goes through her large purse and pulls out a cutout news article attached to a clipboard. "And will be again."

Giovanna lets us know how she's connecting the Folly Beach Public Market, situated downtown in the public park, with the Gullah community's market.

"I see myself as a cultural bridge."

I ask if any of the families on this point were white. She gives me a funny look but then answers.

"There have been some white families on this land, and one family still on it, but mostly they keep to their end and we keep to ours."

She stands to go.

"It's friendly, though. We are there for each other when it's needed."

After ordering dinner, my mom and I slip outside and walk out to the end of the spit of land. It's a lovely evening, just now getting a little nippy as the sun drops behind the marsh. On our way back, my mom says hey to an older man standing with his lady friend in the doorway of the club, which is not yet open for the night's business.

"Hey, you came!"

It's the man who told her about the place earlier that day! He seems surprised and genuinely pleased.

We wander back, drawn by the aromatics mixing with the salt marsh smells. When the dinner arrives, everyone quiets down to get to the serious business of eating. The food is tasty. Ali orders the low-country shrimp. There are at least two sides of ribs, a little pulled pork. A seafood platter. Another rounds of drinks. The table stops talking for a while in that universal sign of approval: the food's just too good for conversation.

The place starts to empty out. Brother Bill joins me outside as the bill gets settled.

There's a skittish, sketchy mutt lurking nearby under a tree. We leave it alone. Funky hip-hop seeps from a car further down the lot, bass pulsing like a tide. Men are scattered about, talking in pairs, leaning against cars. We pass a row of young men, all hip-hop swagger and cool car bravado. I put my hand out at my side, fingers splayed, as a way to say *hey*. One guy gives a nod to acknowledge our presence—not friendly but not hostile either.

More young men arrive in their tricked out cars, revving and posturing, eager to take back their spot and convert it to their late night scene. As we head back to our group, I do my best to give off a quiet confidence, one that whispers, *We're happy to be here, won't take anything or try too hard, just enjoying the breeze and booze and the cool scene. Thanks for sharing it all with us for this one evening.*

Field

Ripton, VT

I'd just laid my head on the pillow, having slipped back to my room for a quick nap, when the mower started up with a roar under my window. It kept up for an entire hour, moving further away from the building, its helicopter chop receding, then trolling back into full volume. I was up on the mountain as a guest, a day into my two-day stay, already a little undone by the social butterflying required by this famous writers' conference that has been, so much, a part of my life. I'd been coming up the mountain ever since I was sixteen, a young aspiring writer visiting his father for a long weekend. A decade has passed since I last participated.

My first attempt at a solo walk down to the river was thwarted by a good-natured attendee eager to share his own introvert's sense of being off-balance. I went back for a second trek after lunch, making it to the edge of the field without incident. Two steps into the woods and the air around me went still, the noisy wind subsiding. Passing through the field, I hadn't quite noticed the racket. But as soon as I backed out onto the edge of the grassy lake, a rush of wind enveloped me, as if someone had turned up a dimmer switch. Two steps back into the forest and everything dropped into silence again. Though not really *silence*, for the river soon got mixed in, gradually immersing me in its liquid music as I stepped carefully down the root-rutted path.

I ended up in the river atop a huge, flat rock off the main path. Slowly taking off my shoes, pulling off my socks, and lying down against the rock face, I let the operating system shut down and the body reboot.

The first night up on the mountain, a long-anticipated storm had hit, dropping down a safety gate of rain on our heads. A mad dash for the dining hall, and a group of half-strangers arrived at our seats drenched, laughing, flush with adrenaline.

On the second evening, my last, I sat on the small hill at the end of the recently mowed lawn, looking down on the campus as night lowered its curtain. I tried and failed to take a panorama shot on my camera phone. What I thought to be a chair in the middle of the grass—with two darkened tracks leading up to it as if it had been dragged there—turned out to be a woman approaching. She was in search of the same view I commanded.

Later, I ended up on a porch overlooking the wild field just up from the river. A few voices leaked out from inside. Someone was tending a fire built as if to conjure an early fall chill not yet fully manifested. The ice in my glass settled down into its mini bathtub of single malt. Inside, talk was of this reading, that workshop. One young man said, "They're well-meaning, with their Black Lives Matter signs on their yards, but, really, they don't know how to act around people of color."

I raised my glass in mock toast. In front of me and above me, peeking out from the porch's overhang, the stars were pinpricking the pulsating night sky; and all around me, it seemed, perched on a corner of the many-acre field, that the grass thrilled to its own audience, a vast single organism; and it may have been the whiskey, but the sky seemed enthralled by the dark and by the quiet wind that inhabited it, moving like a dancer carrying a tray of empty glasses through a crowd of bystanders. I felt that I could step out into it all, weightless, a stripped husk, could twirl out into it like an ash riding eddies, and that no one would know I'd ever been there or, if they did, wouldn't care if I never returned.

Flood

The grass is drenched with last night's downpour; the dogs pass through it like kids running in feathery snow. Up above the riverbank, the jabber of crows.

The news from Puerto Rico has been filling television screens for days. The lack of immediate response from the Administration reminds me of Bush and Hurricane Katrina. Hard to believe it's been more than a decade since Katrina sent heavy rains and evacuees up our way. I remember trying to imagine what it would be like trapped there—no car, no money, no way out. We'd put Avery on our back, we said, and just start walking out. But, of course, we'd have the money to drive out. Could skip the endless lines up and down the coast. No help arriving any time soon.

And what did Asheville face and will again? Heavy rains, maybe some flooding. Our response? Guilty for being so lucky, sending money and blankets.

There is a virtue, I must presume, in shamelessness, since by placing on parade the things one does not know, one discovers that no one else knows either.

—Robert Ardrey

Lightness

Kokomo, IN

We've been driving all day, on our way up to Northern Michigan for vacation. Avery has been hooked up to his YouTube IV-drip for hours and needs to get some exercise. Everyone's famished. Luckily, there's a decent restaurant across the street from the hotel. *Where are we?* Avery asks. *Nowhere, Indiana.*

I wake early in the musty hotel room, hungover from last night's strong drinks. Ali is snoring lightly as I gather up my things and make my way outside, bound for the Starbucks I spied the night before. I walk on the industrial road behind the hotel; three times I have to move out of the way of some asshole speeding to work. It's not yet seven in the morning.

There are half a dozen SUVs in line in the drive-thru pit stop and two more zooming around looking for the right angle of entry. When I ask for my dark roast in a ceramic mug, the barista gives me a dull look. No one looks up from his or her laptop. Feeling like a ghost from some bygone era, I head outside. I plop down at a table on the empty patio facing the road, and the night's concluding dream rises up inside the coffee steam.

In the dream I am naked, or near naked, walking through a festive scene, ashamed of my exposed appearance. Hoping to get away from the crowd, I pass down into a cement tunnel. There's a metal door at its end, but it is locked. I walk back to the tunnel opening. The door has been closed and locked behind me. Getting a little panicky, I hurry back to the first door, hoping that, this time, it will be unlocked. And it is, but it opens to a brick wall. The room starts to shrink. I am still inside the dream but have the presence of mind to say to myself, opening and closing my eyes rapidly: "This must end!" And so it does. Finally, I am freed from the claustrophobic space.

Eventually I head back to the hotel, once again avoiding the speeding, impatient cars with their anonymous drivers. Restaurant workers and a few other uniformed souls mill outside a Texas Roadhouse. I give Ali and Avery a light wake-up shake and grab another coffee in the lobby. I will wait for them to come down. *Get me out of this strip mall hell!*

There are no empty tables, so I drag a chair against a wall and hunker down with Italo Calvino's *Six Memos for the Next Millennium*. I forget why I brought this particular book along on the trip. But its first essay is entitled "Lightness," so I start reading. I can't help but be acutely aware of the people around me, chatting, chowing down breakfast, preparing to get back on the road. *I hate these awful people*, I think, wishing the lobby all to myself. Maybe Calvino, with his treatise on lightness, will lift me out of this existential hissy fit.

Calvino quotes a story of a certain poet-philosopher, Guido Cavalcanti, which appears in Boccaccio's *The Decameron*: "One day, Guido left Orto San Michele and walked along the Corso degli Adimari, which was often his route, as far as San Giovanni. Great marble tombs . . . were . . . scattered about . . . As he was standing between the porphyry columns . . . Messer Betto and his company came riding along . . . Catching sight of Guido among the tombs, they said, 'Let's go and pick a quarrel.' Spurring their horses, they came down upon him in play, like a charging squad, before he was aware of them. They began: 'Guido, you refuse to be of our company; but look, when you have proved that there is no God, what will you have accomplished?' Guido, seeing himself surrounded by them, answered quickly: 'Gentlemen, you may say anything you wish to me in your own home.' Then resting his hand on one of the great tombs and being very nimble, he leaped over it and, landing on the other side, made off and rid himself of them."

Calvino points out the doubled lightness of Cavalcanti's reaction. For, not only does he nimbly avoid the bullying goon squad but also insults them first by calling the tombs their "home." Whereas he is light and alive—now you see him, now you don't—they are leaden and dead.

As I look around me and watch the crowd go through its road-trip machinations, it strikes me that the Boccaccio story matches the scene—in utero—of me walking down that business road from hotel to Starbucks and back. As if reading my mind, Calvino writes: "Maybe I was only then becoming aware of the weight, the inertia, the opacity of the world—the qualities that stick to writing from the start, unless one finds some way of evading them."

Clearly, I need to lighten up.

"Were I to choose an auspicious image for the new millennium," Calvino muses, "I would choose that one: the sudden agile leap of the poet-philosopher who raises himself above the weight of the world, showing that, with all his gravity, he has the secret of lightness, and that what many consider to be the vitality of the times—noisy, aggressive, revving and roaring—belongs to the realm of death, like a cemetery of rusty cars."

Ali appears with her box of toiletries, dumping them dramatically on a side table. She needs coffee. Avery heads straight for the car, headphones on. I dip back into the book one last time. Calvino concludes: "Lightness for me goes with precision and determination." Then: "Paul Valery said: 'One should be light like a bird, and not like a feather.'"

Clearly, I have a ways to go. Maybe a few hours of highway driving will bring me up to speed. Or maybe, in my dream, with the rapid closing and opening of my eyes—and the utterance "This must end!"—I have already changed the stifling reality of life, sidestepping death in an instinctive act of liveliness. I just haven't caught up with myself yet.

In Deep

Halfway down the concourse you decide to get a massage. Your neck has been killing you, thrown out of whack by a week of hauling furniture. Spying the massage chairs, you swerve in. The woman behind the spa-on-the-go counter has a look on her face you can only read as open disdain. You think, *One more rich guy requiring a massage.*

"Swedish or deep tissue?"

You hesitate for a moment, not sure what you should choose.

"Deep tissue?"

The young woman smiles crisply and looks behind her.

"Hey, Candice," she calls out, almost gleefully. "This gentleman wants a Deep."

Candice takes a minute to fit you in the massage chair, but, soon enough, she has her elbow underneath your scapula, and you are bracing with your legs so the chair doesn't spill you onto the carpeted floor.

Fifteen minutes later, you're back at the counter. The woman takes one look at your face and laughs.

"She kill you?"

It has been a rough, painful, but largely therapeutic massage.

"Yeah, she killed me."

The woman jams the receipt down on the metal spike. "Hey Candy?!"

Candice looks up from cleaning around the chair.

"He dead."

Want That!

Frankfort, MI

A middle-aged woman pushes an elderly man in a wheelchair. I am sitting on a bench, watching over Ellen's golden retriever, Callie.

"Can he pat him?" the woman asks, smiling.

"Sure, but, watch out, she might take off an arm."

The man reaches out to the dog and pats the thick, wet-from-the-lake fur. He looks to be in his early seventies, dark-pink, suntanned skin wrinkled and spotted. He says something, but I can't understand him. The daughter makes a strange set of hand and mouth gestures, with one quick eye roll, that she hopes described the situation.

"She could be a therapy dog," I tell her, realizing as I say it that the remark has social problems. *And what about that torn-off arm quip, anyway?*

The man is saying something again, so I look into his eyes and let him talk. I nod and smile but remain unable to interpret his mumbled words. It doesn't really matter. He grabs hold of my wrist; I lean in. The daughter, eager to move on, pulls away her father's hand. He resists, literally putting his foot down.

"Have a good day," the daughter says, a slight frown on her face. Turning in his seat, reaching out, the man springs clear of his mumbling haze. He declares, clear as day, pointing to Callie: "Want that!"

The daughter breaks into laughter. I want to see the look on her face, but father and daughter have already moved on.

Regional

I first spy him in front of the airport's huge regional map. He is focusing intently, arms at his sides, at the mountains somewhere west of Asheville.

I run into him again in line to board the plane. He's older, lean, with white close-cropped hair, dressed in the garb of an old-time farmer—plaid shirt, baggy khaki pants held up by suspenders. His teeth are chewing-tobacco brown. He greets me with eyes wide open behind round spectacles.

And so, when he sits down beside me on the plane, I wait until he settles to ask: "Where were you on the map?"

It takes him a moment to figure my meaning.

"Haywood County."

He pulls out a small ice pack, inside a Ziploc bag, and places it down the back of his shirt.

"How long you live there?"

"All my life."

I ask him what town he lives closest to, and he answers, "Waynesville."

Then, a few beats later: "When I walk Main Street, downtown, I feel like I am on vacation. Boy, I've seen that town *change*."

Turns out he worked as a tool-and-dye man for thirty-eight years. In Asheville. That he has lived on the same mountain farm since he was a boy. He says it used to be farmland, but now it's just pasture and woodland.

"All I do is garden and mow."

"Where you headed?"

He turns in his seat. "Mayo Clinic. Rochester, Minnesota."

Before I can ask, he confesses: "Had a liver transplant twenty years ago. Gone back every year since."

He sees the same people every year, he says, including the drivers who shuttle him from hotel to clinic and back.

His mother, age eighty-nine, used to join him on these trips, but this year is the third year she has stayed behind. The travel became too difficult.

"Siblings?"

"One brother. He lives down the mountain away. It's just me and Mom. My father died young. So I took on . . . the manly things."

He says this quietly, not looking at me. A smile fissures across his face. Then: "But Mom is still in charge."

"She'll be alone while you're gone?"

"Neighbors will look in on her."

He adds, visibly upset: "The television went out last night. It worries me."

We fall silent. He turns to Sudoku.

When our short flight is close to over, I ask again about the transplant. He places the ice pack back in his bag along with the Sudoku book. He arranges himself in his seat. Throws me a furtive glance.

"They fixed that problem. Now I have others."

Exhibit A

Only halfway through the first room of David Hockney's portrait exhibit at LACMA, and, all of a sudden, I realize that Hockney's endless parade of awkward white men seated in pastel armor is really a manifesto of privilege. Even the few people of color he has sit for him, the maybe dozen women, have been airbrushed into white men, gentiles, set inside a stultifying rectangle of nostalgic high society posing as royalty.

I stop before entering the next room, admitting that I am bored silly by these paintings, which are really the same painting painted over and over. (And are they really painted at all?) Whiteness is not just a construct but a grand conspiracy concocted to keep everyone not already grandfathered in from crashing the gates.

This is not an exhibit; it's an advertisement for life in some asshole's inner circle, one big *Fuck you* to the commoners shuffling through.

My response? *Fuck you too*. And walk on out.

At the elevators, two women are waiting for the doors to open. They are dressed sharply and weighted down by bags.

I can't help myself. "How'd you like the show?"

They look at each other. What do they say to this possibly over-friendly white guy?

"Um . . . it was good."

I nod my head and bite my lip.

The doors open and I step inside.

One asks: "What did *you* think?"

"I hated it," I say, pushing the button. "Just a bunch of rich white people in a row."

Both women laugh out loud as the doors close.

Quarter

Sunday afternoon and nearly all the machines are chock-full of spinning, churning clothes, towels, sheets. The young man in yoga pants and an old T-shirt is lifting out yoga pants and old T-shirts from the washer and draping them over the wheeled laundry basket's overhanging bar. An older, jumpsuited woman with an echo of a cigarette on her lip drags a plastic tub of sodden curtains to the open mouth of a dryer.

Another woman, much younger, dour of expression, sits on a bench engrossed in her smartphone, empty garbage bags gaping at her feet; three young boys gallop around a bank of dryers and pass around her like a raging river slipping over boulders. She keeps scrolling, unperturbed. Clanking away, two change machines on the wall dispense quarters . . . five . . . ten . . . twenty. Above, a big-screen television mounted on the wall broadcasts *Law & Order*, sound down low. A clutch of bored souls lounges in a line of scuffed rocking chairs, not so much watching the show as absorbing its aura.

We've been without washer and dryer for weeks and will be for the foreseeable future while the renovation project invents new ways to sabotage itself—new permits required, workers injured, roof leaks sprung. It's been more than a decade since I've hauled dirty clothes out of my car, purchased little rectangular boxes of detergent, or spoon-fed quarters into ancient, leaking machines. And I kind of like it. Along with the pick-up basketball court and the DMV line, the laundry attracts its own little democracy.

Soccer moms dump three children's worth of sports garb in a jumbo washer. Construction workers arrive in pairs. A waitress I recognize from a pizza place up the street toils over a gigantic pile of unfolded clothes, an unlit cigarette behind one ear. I am most intrigued, however, by the dapper gentleman dressed to the nines standing by as his single load of tri-color towels whirls and twirls. What's he doing, cleaning up after a murder?

I retreat to my car. There's a guy taking a piss in a stand of trees. A righteous young couple sits in their outfitted van—not quite hippy, more utilitarian festival—facing each other, legs crossed, parallel playing on their laptops. I've got room in my hatchback to create my own portable study, and a gallon of warm water to swig off. Twenty-two minutes to go before I head back inside and introduce myself to the bank of dryers.

Now I'm standing by, impatiently waiting for the last load. One of the women who works here is going from dryer to dryer, pushing a wheeled laundry basket, dumping coin boxes one after the other into a plastic tub. She has a key attached to a chain that she turns to open the box, which slides right out. The steady cascade of coins pries two girls from their floor drawing to see what's up.

"That's a good sound," I say, trying not to hover behind the woman menacingly.

"Yup," she says, not looking my way. "Sure is."

She moves onto the next pair of machines but pauses mid-key. Looks over at me.

"I always try to listen . . ." she puts a finger up to her ear, tapping it lightly, ". . . for that sound . . ."

I smile at her, though not sure yet what she means.

". . . I listen for that one silver sound." She turns back to her work. "One quarter is usually pure silver, you know."

Key in slot, box slid out, dumped in the tub.

I listen for the silver sound but can only hear the dull roar of coins dropping from their chute. The woman nods in my direction, back in her work groove, bumping the basket with her thigh to get it rolling again.

She opens the next box, the next.

Zombieland

You need three houses or three jobs to live here.
—*a Sun Valley saying*

The place looks like a set for an apocalyptic movie or the site of a survivalist compound shootout—two abandoned SUVs in the driveway, tires flat, and a wind-downed sapling drooped against the front door awning.

You peer inside: a soccer ball has come to rest at a basket of laundry. Dishes are stacked on a counter; the dust coating piles of boxes and hoarder mind spreads like mold.

You can imagine the man—estranged from his family, wife long moved out—one day in the act of putting water on for coffee, saying to himself *Fuck it!* He puts the kettle down and turns off the flame, then heads for the door, grabbing a hat in the foyer. He stops and turns at the fence for one last look, long enough to curse the property, hand flapped out in a disgusted wave. *I'm outta here.*

Five years later. The fence has fallen to the ground, scrub oaks have taken over. What sold for $1.2 million now only a line item on some bookkeeper's ledger. Neighbors' property values plunging.

You wonder if the guy's just out of the country. Or maybe his wife came out to the property one day and shot him, buried him out back; maybe she took the money in the safe, then hightailed it out of there. Either way, raccoons have taken up residence in the rusty Suburban out front.

Festival

Black Mountain, NC

The opening night campers are settling into their end-of-the-evening modes. I'm lying in my tent; Avery and his pal, one tent over, whisper of late night escapades. Someone starts pounding on a board. A man chants loudly in what I presume to be Cherokee. He knocks on the board and chants. Quiet.

I can hear a guitar faintly playing a folk tune; laughter further up the field. I'm on my back, looking through the mesh at the top of my tent. Now someone's started telling a story, slowly, earnestly. I can barely make out the words but imagine listeners circled around a fire.

A couple plows close by our tents, drunk. One says to the other, "Camping is cheating, but a cabin is extra cheating."

A tent neighbor coughs the first of a night's worth of coughs. Then the knocking board. Then the chant again, each word or phrase enunciated with precision. To me, a mix of pride and sadness. Then back to the story.

As I listen, understanding little, taking it all in, my body slowly releases the various tightnesses of the day, and my breath, garaged car, ticks down to sleep.

Merging

"Never arrive in a city in the middle of rush hour," the novelist proclaimed in the travel essay I was reading. Halfway through the piece, and almost at the end of my flight, the line ran in front of my eyes. In mere minutes, my plane would touch down at Newark airport—at 5:03 p.m., precisely the time the pilot announced, twice, we would be landing. And soon after that, after a somnambulant trek from gate to terminal entrance to curb, just my luck, the cab would plow right into snarled traffic, slowing to a crawl just outside the blocked artery of the Holland tunnel, the cabbie making a mad, last-second swerve into the dwindling lanes, causing the cars behind to honk irritably.

With time to kill, I began to ask the man questions. He was from Egypt, had lived in Jersey for over twenty years. His wife had resided with him for over a decade, though they still had extended family back in Cairo—actually, a suburb just outside the city. He kept his cab immaculately clean as a matter of pride, as a daily practice.

"Come on," he called to the drivers crowding us from behind. "We must merge."

He gestured with both hands at the road ahead. "It's what we are doing here, good people—merging!"

Shooter

Sitting here in my car, once again waiting for my boy to get out of school—though Avery's no longer a boy, and *school* is high school. At three thirty the doors will knock open and students will stream out, heading up the hill—some climbing into waiting cars, some (the seniors!) making for their own cars, others walking home or to work or to practice.

I come early to nab a spot up front, happy to wait for the gift of getting to drive out unencumbered. I bring my work, a book, a crossword, or I read the news on my phone. If the weather is good, I roll down the windows and play some music, or I abandon the car and walk circles along the outside of the upper lot. When it's cold, I hunker down, engine turned off, and focus on the work at hand.

But on days like today, the one-year anniversary of the Parkland shooting, all I can think of is an "active" shooter appearing at one of the doors—of students running and screaming from the building, of cop cars pulling up, the sound of automatic gunfire. I can't help imagining the scene, wondering what I would do in such a moment, what any of us in our cars would do.

When I calm down and bring myself back to the lazy, slow afternoon, I begin to wonder what makes someone *become* a mass shooter. About the conditions it takes. And I don't buy the line that these men— so often *young* men—act alone, that they are mentally unstable. They may be, in fact, mentally unstable, or battling trauma, or, in some way, out of their right mind, but our culture has helped make them this way, primed them to be violent in this way. Brainwashed, they come out of a *specific* situation, environment, training ground.

■ ■ ■

The students start streaming out of the school. One of the teachers puts on a traffic vest and starts waving cars forward. I search the crowd, finally spotting Avery as he hikes up the grassy hill outside the old gym. He's grown so much. Has come so far from the eight-year-old boy who climbed out of that ruined car unsure if his parents were going to make it. It 's hard to believe that seven years have passed.

Avery spots the car and heads my way. He looks into the side window to make sure he has chosen the right silver Subaru, flipping his hair unconsciously before he opens the door and climbs in.

"Hey, Dad."

He plugs in his phone and turns up the hip-hop.

Acknowledgments

The author would like to thank the editors of the following publications in which some of these micro essays first appeared:

American Poetry Review: "Across the Tracks"; *The Common:* "Boxes" (online), "Close," "Invisible" (online); *Connotations:* "Blue Nude," "For Lady V," "Notes from the Strip"; *Enchanting Verses Review:* "Improvise"; *Shadowgraph:* "Her Hair"; *Slag City Review:* "Gospel"; and *Valparaiso Review:* "Wild"

The following pieces appeared in the Asheville-based online arts and culture magazine *Asheville Grit:* "Blind Spot," "Determined," "Festival," "Living Large at Snapper Jack's," "No Trespassing," "Useless," and "At the Waterpark."

"Regional" first appeared in the Asheville-based online arts and culture magazine *Holler Asheville.* Many of these pieces first turned up on my blog, *Stolen Moments.*

Thanks to: Gary Clark and everyone at Vermont Studio Center; Dr. Charles Rowell and everyone at *Callaloo*; Ali McGee at the *Grit*; Gary Hawkins and Landon Godfrey; Jeri Augusto at Brown's Center for Racial Justice; Gregory Pardlo; Fred D'Guair; Ryan Walsh; Ailish Hopper; Nicole Sealey; Sarah Gambito; Deborah Paredez; Jon Davis; Jody Gladding; Oliver Bendorf; John Wood; Alexandria Ravenel and Building Bridges of Asheville; Alexander Long; Catina Bacote and Carl Roberts; Beth Ann Fennelly; Kris Hartum and Dave Burr at The Talking Book; Patrick Phillips; Jerriod Avant; Kazim Ali; Gerry LaFemina; Garrett Hongo; Dana Levin; Micah Mead, Diana Finch; Barry Sanders; Jay Wherley; Marie Harris and

Charter Weeks; Christopher Merrill; Susan Steinberg; and Kevin McIlvoy.

Holly Watson at Holly Watson PR.

Kate Gale, Mark Cull, Tobi Harper, Monica Fernandez, Natasha McClellan, and the entire Red Hen Press team.

And, as always, Ali and Avery.

Biographical Note

Sebastian Matthews is the author of a memoir, *In My Father's Footsteps*, and two books of poetry, *We Generous* and *Miracle Day*. His hybrid collection of poetry and prose, *Beginner's Guide to a Head-On Collision*, won the Independent Publisher Book Awards' silver medal. Matthews is also the author of the collage novel, *The Life & Times of American Crow*. His work has appeared in or on, among other places, *The Atlantic, Blackbird, The Common, Georgia Review, Poetry Daily, Poets & Writers, The Sun, Virginia Quarterly Review*, and the *Writer's Almanac*. Learn more at sebastianmatthews.com.